10-Minute Time and Stress Management

10-Minute Time and Stress Management

HOW TO GAIN AN 'EXTRA' 10 HOURS A WEEK!

Dr DAVID LEWIS

PIATKUS

Copyright © 1995 by David Lewis

First published in 1995 by
Judy Piatkus (Publishers) Ltd of
5 Windmill Street, London W1P 1HF

Reprinted 1995
First paperback edition 1995

The moral rights of the author have been asserted

*A catalogue record for this book is available
from the British Library*

ISBN 0-7499-1428-9 hbk
ISBN 0-7499-1536-6 pbk

Designed by Chris Warner

Typeset by Action Typesetting, Gloucester
Printed and bound in Great Britain by
Mackays of Chatham PLC, Chatham, Kent

CONTENTS

Acknowledgements

My grateful thanks to the following busy people who still found time to give me their practical ideas for time management. They are, in alphabetical order: Jeffrey Archer; Rosemary Conley, chairman of Rosemary Conley Diet and Fitness Clubs; Denys Henderson, chairman of ICI and Zeneca; Colin Marshall, chairman of British Airways; David Paistow, chairman of Inchcape; Bob Reed, chairman, British Railways Board; Stephen Rubin, chairman of the Pentland Group; Geoff Shingles, chairman of Digital; Martin Taylor, vice-chairman of the Hanson Trust; Peter Walters, chairman, Midland Bank, Blue Circle and Smith Kline Beecham.

My thanks are also due to my researcher, Mandy Bruce, for her valuable assistance, and to Cynthia Hemming, managing director of the David Lewis Consultancy, for her – as always – useful suggestions.

PREFACE: AN EVEN SHORTER HISTORY OF TIME

IN MEDIEVAL EUROPE time was regulated by the church, which laid down rules about what could and could not be done on specific days. Canons required the recital of prayers at definite times of the day: Matins before dawn, Prime at sunrise and Nones at nine. Later, Nones moved to mid-day giving us 'noon'. These Canonical 'hours' did not mean a period of sixty minutes but less precise parts of the day set aside for praying.

Although the first mechanical clocks were built around 1300 (before then sand and water clocks were widely used) they remained little more than a status symbol for centuries. Even an important 17th-century government official like Samuel Pepys organised his day by means of a sundial and church bells (the word 'clock' is derived from 'clocca', the Latin for 'bell').

The modern idea of time arose out of Puritan opposition to the Roman Catholic ecclesiastical calendar. Their notion of six working days, followed by a day of rest, had been generally adopted by the end of the 17th century.

In an agricultural society, where seasons dictated the pace of life, there was little need to measure time with any great accuracy.

As late as the reign of George II (1727–60), travel was no faster than it had been during the first century BC. All this changed after 1784, when John Palmer, the MP for Bath, introduced Britain's first public transport system which ran to a strict timetable. His stage coaches left Bath in the late afternoon, drove through the night and reached Lombard Street general post office by 8 a.m. the following day.

At this time, all towns set their clocks by local or sun time, which meant that Falmouth in the West Country might be 20 minutes behind London, while Norwich was seven minutes ahead. Because of this, the first stage coaches carried time pieces set to lose or gain as required.

Even after a national railway network was established, attitudes remained relaxed. When George Bradshaw was compiling his first railway timetable, in 1839, one railway company declined to provide any arrival times, objecting that: 'It would tend to make punctuality a sort of obligation.'

When the St Stephen's Tower, which contains London's most famous bell, Big Ben (named after Boxer Benjamin Caunt, who weighed 238lb at his last fight), was completed in 1856, the Astronomer Royal, Sir George Airy, insisted its clocks be set to Greenwich Mean Time. Within a short time all Britain's clocks followed suit.

In industrial towns and cities, where a giant clock above the mill or factory often marked time for an entire community, crafty bosses were not above ensuring their time pieces ran slow during the working day and speeded up once the factory closed. To prevent their ploy being discovered, employees were banned from bringing watches on to the premises. From this comes the tradition of presenting a long-serving worker with a watch or clock on retirement, symbolising the fact that 'time' is finally their own.

Today, few people enjoy that luxury. In all advanced industrial nations, time has become an increasingly scarce resource and time deprivation one of its most serious problems. When listening to hard-pressed managers, professionals and self-employed people recounting their time pressure woes, I am often reminded of these lines by A.A. Milne, creator of Winnie the Pooh:

> *'Here is Edward Bear coming downstairs now, bump, bump, bump on the back of his head behind*

Christopher Robin. It is, so far as he is aware, the only way of coming down the stairs. Although sometimes he feels there must be a better way, if only he could stop bumping his head long enough to think about it.'

These days, not many people in business are able to stop bumping their heads long enough to work out how coming downstairs might be a more rewarding, less painful, experience.

It was with this consideration in mind that I developed 10-Minute Time and Stress Management. This programme contains four elements:

1　Practical procedures which explain HOW you can manage your time more efficiently.

2　The ideas which underpin each procedure, and describe WHY a particular approach is suggested.

3　Background information and examples to provide a broader perspective on key issues of time management and our attitudes towards time.

4　Exercises you need to complete in order to benefit from this programme.

Only by completing them will you understand how and why your time is currently being wasted and what practical steps you can take to use it more profitably.

As an aid to efficient reading, glance quickly through each chapter before reading it thoroughly; you will in this way prepare your brain for the ideas and information it contains. (Research shows that such preparation greatly enhances comprehension, retention and recall.)

In today's pressured society, managing your time efficiently is not merely useful, it is essential. On this skill depends:

- Whether or not you achieve your goals in life.
- Whether or not your deadlines are met.
- Whether your work is productive and fulfilling, or pressured and frustrating.

The secret of managing your time is to work not harder but more efficiently. This book provides you with the knowledge to do just that.

INTRODUCTION: THE TIME AND STRESS CRISIS

'Now, here, you see, it takes all the running you can do, to keep in the same place. If you want to get somewhere else, you must run at least twice as fast as that!'

Lewis Carroll – *Through the Looking Glass*

LET ME INTRODUCE YOU to a young acquaintance of mine – Chris. I think you may find you have common interests.

Chris came into the office an hour early to tackle a mountain of urgent paper work. Intimidated by the sheer size of the backlog, he found it hard to concentrate or decide his priorities. As a result, by the time other staff arrived, his sole accomplishment had been to transform that mountain into several smaller mounds. For the rest of the day, constant interruptions – by subordinates seeking guidance, colleagues needing to discuss departmental projects, demands from his superiors, endless telephone calls and unscheduled visitors – meant he made little further progress in catching up with his work. Twelve hours after his working day had started, an exhausted and demoralised Chris left for home, with the backlog almost unchanged.

Sound familiar? Welcome to the world of overwork!

Racing against time

No matter what job you do or position you hold, the chances are that, like Chris, you find yourself in a losing race against time. Despite putting in longer and longer hours, more people are finding workplace demands continue to escalate, and, with them, experiencing rising levels of stress. In fact, societies in Europe, the USA and Japan are all currently facing crises of time and stress; and by the turn of the century, these pressures are likely to present both employees and employers with the greatest threats to their personal well-being and corporate performance.

Ironically, not long ago some futurologists – the same ones who, I suspect, were busy predicting a paperless office – boldly forecast the imminent arrival of an age of leisure. According to them, we were fast approaching a golden era in human history, in which our main concern would be finding ways of spending unlimited free time!

As we know to our cost, things did not work out like that. Following mergers, 'downsizing' and recessionary cost cutting, many employees now find it difficult to get even a day off or to leave for home before the cleaners arrive. No matter how much they yearn for a more balanced life, most are obliged to sacrifice personal and family life to gain promotion or even to safeguard their jobs. Over the past 20 years, working hours have gone up. In the United States, they have increased by the equivalent of an extra month per year; time spent commuting has risen by a full day each year, while holidays are down by three-and-a-half days. Recent surveys also suggest many European and North American white-collar workers are now approaching the Japanese tradition of 12-hour days and work-filled evenings.

When Priority Management, Seattle based consultants, polled more than a thousand US middle managers, they found over half routinely working between 50 and 60 hours per week, with 6 per cent putting in even more time.

As a result, it has been calculated that the average man or

woman in their thirties now has only 30 minutes a day to call their own. Yet despite the long hours, four out of 10 middle managers still have more work to do than time to do it in, which helps to explain why Priority Management also reported 85 per cent worried that they were spending too little time with their families.

So many pressures

While some managers thrive on the challenge posed by longer hours, especially if they have the power to make decisions and regulate their schedule, many others find the pressures hard to endure. One Chief Executive described the workplace as a marathon race in which a minority manage to spring across the finishing line, while the majority fall exhausted by the wayside. Just how many employees burn out behind the front runners depends to some extent on the corporate culture. If senior managers view a worker's productivity in terms of quality rather than merely the number of hours worked, pressures are usually more manageable.

Unfortunately, intense global competition, and entrenched ideas about what it takes to be a 'team player', mean the majority of organisations continue to equate efficiency, loyalty and ambition with the length of the working day.

In one major US company, for example, the managing director, who prides himself on being first to arrive and last to leave, walks around the staff car park at 7 a.m. feeling the radiators of senior executives' cars. If these are warm, indicating recent arrival, the owners may find a black mark on their records.

This insidious combination of increasing hours, heavier workloads, loss of security, personal debt and rising aspirations has sent levels of work-related stress soaring. According to Professor Cary Cooper, of the University of Manchester Institute of Science and Technology, stress levels have more than doubled in the past seven years. He found more than half of all company chairmen and senior executives, in one of his surveys, suffered from hours-related stress.

The result is an unprecedented rise in stress-related health problems, including coronary heart disease, ulcers, high blood pressure, weakened immune systems, strokes, depression and emotional breakdown. In Japan, where employees work an average of 400 hours a year more than their European counterparts, a powerful work ethic, strong company loyalty and intense competition have led to a virtual epidemic of *karoshi*, or 'death from overwork'. So many workers – not only corporate executives, but bus and taxi drivers, sales people, journalists, doctors and nurses – have, fallen victim to *karoshi* that a recent survey found 40 per cent of white collar employees fear they will be killed by their jobs.

The time famine

Twenty-five years ago, in *The Harried Leisure Classes*, Steffan Linder prophesied that economic development would produce a 'time famine' in advanced societies. He warned that as time pressures increased, such leisurely pursuits as relaxing over a meal or taking quiet country walks would be replaced by activities that could be completed at speed. Today, with fast food and jogging, his prediction has been largely fulfilled. From microwaved convenience foods to high speed elevators, technology aids and abets our demands for everything 'now'.

Fred Hirsch, another prophet of the 1970s, predicted in *The Social Limits of Growth* that time starvation would create an increasingly alienated and less sociable society. 'Friendliness,' he cautioned, 'is time consuming and thereby liable to be economised because of its extravagant absorption of this increasingly scarce input.'

With so many pressures on home and family life, it is hardly surprising that many marriages, relationships and individuals are coming apart at the seams. Nor is it any wonder that in some of the most pressured companies productivity is declining alongside morale, motivation and performance.

To aggravate matters still further, it is becoming increasingly apparent that gruelling hours and high stress levels are not just a short-term difficulty but a permanent feature of working life. There are three compelling reasons why this should be so.

1 Reduced staffs – increased demands

Whether it is called 'downsizing', 'delayering', 'rationalisation' or, as one euphemism for dismissing staff puts it, 'freeing up their options', the end result is fewer staff coping with ever increasing work pressures. It is a trend set to continue, as old style, vertical corporate management hierarchies are replaced by horizontally organised companies, designed to ensure more efficient communications and faster response times.

2 Reduced resources – increased productivity

To achieve both reduced costs and increased productivity, more and more human skills are being replaced by automation. Relentless advances in technology make this an accelerating trend. Just as robots have eliminated many blue collar assembly line jobs, so will new generations of computers eliminate many white collar jobs. To give one example: voice recognition technology may eliminate the need for secretaries, as executives can dictate letters, reports and memos directly into their desk-top PCs. Moore's Law, formulated several years ago by the co-inventor of the microchip, physicist Gordon Moore, states that raw computing power doubles every 18 months.

Its validity is shown by the fact that the musical chip found in low cost greetings cards contain more computing power than existed in the whole world before 1950. The microprocessor controlling an amateur video camera is as powerful as the IBM 360 mainframe that heralded the computing age.

Before long, virtually every machine in the office or factory will be capable of a high degree of self-regulation and control, with the inevitable consequence that fewer carbon-based, warm-blooded life forms will be required by organisations dominated by silicon-based, electronic life forms.

3 Intense global competition – accelerated rates of change

Faced with relentless, international competition, no company can enjoy the luxury of standing still or even pausing to catch its corporate breath. Firms must either change constantly or be changed by the business environment. This pressure for continuous change will become even greater as hungry, highly flexible Pacific Rim and Chinese companies enter the commercial arena. Taiwanese computer manufacturers, for example, have reduced the time taken to develop a new product to 90 days, from drawing board to production line.

The speed of change, with its accompanying stress and demands on time, can only increase, because of three related factors:

- The exponential growth in new information will shortly double every 20 months. This means that additional time must be found constantly to update knowledge and skills.

- The speed at which information becomes obsolete. Not so long ago, knowledge gained during the first 20 years or so of life was sufficient to earn a living for the next 40 years. Today, the vast majority of information has an ever shortening shelf life, a use-by date after which it has little or no marketable value. In computing, for instance, the application of Moore's Law suggests that around half the information possessed by an expert in this field becomes redundant within a couple of years.

- The speed at which information is now communicated. In the recent past, managers had time to reflect on tough decisions, to seek further information, canvas other opinions, and analyse events carefully before reaching their considered judgement. Author Tom Peters recalls how, while he was working at McKinsey and Co, they didn't even bother taking inflation into account while making 20-year cash-flow projections for quarter-billion-dollar petrochemical facilities. They felt that supply, demand, and commodity prices for wheat and corn could be predicted with a fine degree of accuracy over this period.

Those days are gone for ever. In the present climate of intense global competition, Peters believes that, 'if you aren't reorganising pretty substantially once every six to 12 months, you're probably out of step with the times.'

In progressive companies, from retailing to manufacturing, and service industries to the financial sector: 'What have we changed this month – or even this week?' has become the most frequent query at all levels. Between dawn and dusk today, for example, Toyota will have carried out as many as 20 changes on their production lines, many suggested by their blue collar workforce. This is not wheel-spinning or change for the sake of change; it is essential for excellence because other firms are also changing all the time. With the pressure of events crowding in on the average manager, there is seldom time for quiet deliberation. Decisions affecting the whole future of the company have to be made against ever tighter deadlines.

And therein lies a danger. Psychological studies have shown that the stress of decisions that offer both significant risks and substantial benefits may trigger two different levels of mental and physical arousal:

- In *vigilance*, heightened alertness helps us make the most appropriate choice.

- In *hypervigilance*, excess stress results in often catastrophic errors of judgement.

The determining factor is the amount of time available in which to form judgements. The less time there is, the greater the risk that hypervigilance will lead to unreliable choices and inappropriate responses.

For all these reasons, the pressures on managers to perform against the clock are set to intensify.

People who complain 'I haven't got the time . . .' are mistaken. *Everybody has all the time there is*: 168 hours per week, to be spent 60 seconds at a time. Since time cannot be stretched, stored or supplemented, our only solution is to manage it sensibly. To ensure that, in the words of Kipling, we *'fill the unforgiving minute, with sixty seconds' worth of distance run . . .'*

On this single management skill depends not only your success but, conceivably, your mental and physical health.

1 | SELF-MANAGEMENT: THE KEY TO TIME MANAGEMENT

'For tyme ylost may naught recovered be'
Geoffrey Chaucer – *Troilus and Criseyde*

LET'S START with a confession: time management is impossible! No executive, however experienced, has ever managed a single second (if you doubt this, then try to manage the next five minutes). So although, for the sake of convenience, I shall continue to use the phrase 'time management', what we are really exploring are ways of managing yourself and – as far as this is possible – your surroundings, with maximum effectiveness.

Because time management is actually self-management, the barriers to its accomplishment are chiefly negative mental attitudes.

Time management attitude assessment

To check your own attitudes, award one point for every statement below which matches your own beliefs.

1 'I'm a naturally disorganised person.'

2 'The only way to get more done is by working even harder.'

3   'I can be equally productive throughout the day.'

4   'Planning your time removes all the spontaneity from life.'

5   'I need the pressures of deadlines to be fully productive.'

6   'I must achieve complete control over how my time is spent.'

7   'If you want a job done well, you have to do it yourself.'

8   'Delegation is always a great time saver.'

9   'I just don't have enough time to get myself organised.'

10 'Lack of punctuality is a sign of inefficiency or discourtesy.'

Score

0: You have a very positive attitude towards time management and should have no difficulty in carrying out the practical procedures described in this book.

1–3: Although you have a constructive approach to managing time, the few negative attributes that you do possess will tend to hold you back. Read my comments below for each statement you scored.

4–6: Your ability to manage time effectively is being undermined by negative beliefs. Read my comments below for each statement you scored.

7–10: This very high score suggests that your ability to manage your time is being significantly impaired by unhelpful and incorrect beliefs. At present it is likely you are very doubtful that it lies within your power to make life easier and less stressful. But working with the procedures in this book *will* help you to develop a positive attitude towards time management.

My comments for each statement you scored

Belief: '*I'm a naturally disorganised person.*'

Reality: If you never learned self-management while young, you may consider yourself naturally disorganised. The truth is, however, that anyone can learn to organise and manage their time, at any age. All it takes is a readiness to make changes in your life, together with the knowledge of where, when and how those changes need to be made.

Belief: *'The only way to get more done is by working even harder.'*

Reality: Some of the hardest workers are also the worst time managers. Despite their long hours, these overworked and, usually, over-stressed individuals tend to combine low productivity with indifferent quality of output. By confusing 'busyness' with 'business', they resemble the lawyer in Chaucer's *The Canterbury Tales*, who 'while no man seemed as busy as he, he was not as busy as he seemed to be!' Learn to eliminate as much 'busyness' as possible from your life, and replace it with doing business in the most time effective manner possible.

Belief: *'I can be equally productive throughout the day.'*

Reality: Your own experience will confirm that this is just not possible. Even the most efficient workers experience peaks and troughs in their levels of energy and alertness. These natural variations are associated with our inbuilt body clocks. During certain periods during the day – for some it's first thing in the morning, for others late afternoon or evening – we feel energetic, motivated, able to focus clearly on problems and to complete assignments with the least amount of effort. At other times, we are mentally and physically drained, lack motivation, and seem incapable of concentration.

One way of reducing stress and utilising your time more effectively is by scheduling the most demanding tasks for your personal prime time. Ways of doing this will be discussed in Chapter 4.

Belief: *'Planning your time removes all spontaneity from life.'*

Reality: Setting yourself clear goals and priorities need not mean becoming trapped in tediously predictable routine. In fact, by managing your time better you will provide even more opportunities to act impulsively. On a hot summer's day, for example, you may yearn to go home early. But urgent reports to write and meetings to attend make this impossible. Time management might enable you to act on such an impulse more easily because many more tasks will have been completed. By including 'being spontaneous' as a goal in life, you will greatly improve your chances of being able to act on impulse whenever an opportunity arises.

Belief: '*I need the pressure of deadlines to be fully productive.*'

Reality: Some people leave important tasks to the last minute, because it produces an adrenalin rush which can be so exhilarating it becomes addictive. While it is true that a certain amount of adrenalin is necessary to feel motivated and confident, leaving everything to the last minute allows no margin for error should things go wrong. Although a limited amount of adrenalin is usually stimulating, too much poses a threat to one's health.

Belief: '*I must achieve complete control over how my time is spent.*'

Reality: No matter how well organised they are, no one ever achieves complete control over their working day. There are just too many workplace Time Bandits lying in ambush. These include important but unscheduled visitors, telephone calls, demands from co-workers, priorities established by superiors without reference to you, meetings, commuting to see clients, being kept waiting on appointments, and so on.

This does not, however, mean it is futile to exercise as much control as possible over your work. As we shall see in Chapters 5–10, even those Time Bandits who cannot be banished can usually be confined.

Belief: '*If you want a job done well, you have to do it yourself.*'

Reality: If you start out trying to do everything, you will end up doing nothing well. Learning when to delegate or drop a particular task is essential if you are to survive ever increasing demands on your time.

Belief: '*Delegation is always a great time saver.*'

Reality: This is equally erroneous. Delegation only saves time provided you know what, when, how and where to delegate (see Chapter 3). If what you consider delegation is just another name for dumping, you will waste not only your own time but that of the person unfortunate enough to be landed with an inappropriately delegated task.

Belief: '*I just don't have enough time to get myself organised.*'

Reality: This reminds me of the story of a Canadian rancher working flat out to chop down the trees needed to build a cabin before winter snows arrived.

'You should sharpen your axe,' a passing lumberjack advised.

'No time,' gasped the exhausted farmer. 'I'm too busy cutting down these trees!'

This perfectly describes a dilemma facing millions of hard-pressed executives, managers, professionals and self-employed men and women today. While realising there must be more productive ways of dealing with their crushing workload, they never manage to find time to do anything about it. This is one reason the procedures of 10-minute time management prove so helpful. They enable you to 'sharpen your axe' without spending so much time on the task that you become snowed under.

Belief: '*Lack of punctuality is a sign of inefficiency or discourtesy.*'

Reality: While some countries, that is, the USA, Canada, Australia, and those in Europe, are precise in their use of time, this is not so with every culture, a point all those engaged in international trade must never forget. In the Middle East, Latin America and China, for instance, a meeting scheduled for 10 a.m. may not start before 11 a.m. or even noon.

Such a delay does not imply, as it might in the West, discourtesy, inefficiency or disinterest. It is just that their culture looks on time in a more relaxed manner. They adopt *polychronic* time, which involves doing several things almost simultaneously. In most Western countries, by contrast, a *monochronic* attitude is the norm, with tasks given priorities and tackled one after the other. Moving from monochronic to polychronic time can be disorientating, and cause the inexperienced to make mistaken and pejorative judgements about the efficiency and enthusiasm of their hosts.

This is not the only way in which different attitudes towards time can confuse the inexperienced business person. The negotiating process is shorter in the United States, for instance, than in many other countries. American business people, typically, spend far less time in developing relationships and fact-finding than their counterparts in the Pacific Rim. However, they devote much more time to debating, posturing and adopting negotiating positions. In Japan and other Pacific Rim nations, where consensus is highly valued, decision making is far slower as a result.

Identifying your time zones

As well as negative beliefs, your general outlook on life significantly affects the way in which you perceive and seek to manage time. Research by Dr Philip Zimbardo of Stanford University suggests people can live in one (or two) of four different time zones. The assessment below allows you to identify which ones you prefer to spend your life in. Because, thankfully, it is impossible to fit people into precise pigeon holes, you may find more than one of these profiles applies in different situations. For example, you could favour **zone**

four at work, and **zone one** at home or when on holiday. In this case, read my comments under both these headings.

Zone one: I prefer a quiet life, free from too much pressure. I like working at my own pace and adopt a relaxed attitude towards deadlines. My view is that if something doesn't get done exactly on time, does it really matter? I am seldom on time for appointments or especially well-organised.

Zone two: My greatest pleasure is being sociable to friends, dining out in company or going to parties. I often act on impulse and may not always think through the consequences of my actions sufficiently. I would far sooner behave in a spontaneous way than try to plan every detail of my life. I prefer a job with plenty of variety, and where I can see the results of my work fast.

Zone three: I prefer to organise my life carefully and prefer routine to variety. I am careful about my diet, take regular exercise and carry medical and life insurance. I think through my actions carefully before proceeding.

Zone four: I enjoy working to tight deadlines and pride myself on my punctuality. I am generally well organised and work best under pressure. I admit to having difficulty relaxing and enjoy facing a variety of challenges. I tend to arrive for appointments on time but at the last minute.

What your Choice Reveals

Zone one: People in this zone have what is termed a 'present fatalistic' outlook on life. Their philosophy is best summed up by the Spanish word *mañana*. They adopt a relaxed, laid back attitude and prefer to delay decisions as long as possible. If you placed yourself in this zone, an obstacle to better time management could be an inability either to get started or, having begun, to persist in your endeavours. Pay special attention to my remarks on positive and negative delay (see Chapter 4).

Zone two: People living in this zone are termed 'present hedonistic', because they are motivated by the need for rapid rewards and enjoyment. If you placed yourself in this zone, a possible barrier to time management is your dislike of planning and organising. You may postpone urgent but disagreeable tasks in favour of lower priority but more enjoyable activities.

Zone three: People who choose this zone are said to be 'future orientated', because they plan and set long-term career and personal goals. If you place yourself in this zone, the chances are that you already manage yourself and your time reasonably effectively. It will still be possible, however, to fine tune your skills, to manage time even more efficiently.

Zone four: This is the choice of people who are termed 'time conscious'. They enjoy working to deadlines and demand punctuality from themselves and others. If you placed yourself in this zone, you may find it difficult to deal with people who are less punctual or show less urgency in meeting deadlines. An obstacle to improved time management could be the addictive nature of the 'deadline' high described above.

Three steps to managing time

To organise yourself and manage your time successfully, it is essential to know three things:

- The goals you want to achieve in your personal and professional life.
- How your time is currently being spent.
- Ways of investing that time most effectively to achieve your goals.

In the next chapter, I will describe a practical method for keeping account of how your working day is spent.

2 | TAKING STOCK OF YOUR TIME

'Until you can manage your time, it is impossible to manage anything else.'

Peter Drucker, management guru

How did you spend your time at work last week? What goals were you able to accomplish? Which ones did you fail to achieve? How often were you interrupted and for how long? What were the most frequent interruptions? Once interrupted, how long did it take you to refocus on the task at hand?

Why memory tends to be unreliable

Unless you are truly exceptional, the likelihood is that you will have only the vaguest recollection of how your time was invested. And even if you do recall most of what went on, there are two reasons why such memories are liable to be inaccurate:

- Our assessment of time is highly subjective. A dull speech that lasts only 10 minutes still appears to drag on for ever. Time appears to slow at the start of a holiday and speed up alarmingly towards the end.

YOUR DAILY TIME TRACKER

PRIORITY	TIME OF DAY	TASK	TIME TAKEN	HOW TIME MIGHT BE SAVED IN FUTURE

- We seek to safeguard our self-esteem by forgetting such time-wasting distractions as socialising, looking for mislaid documents, lingering over lunch and staring out of the window.

We also prefer to forget occasions when an unpleasant high priority activity was delayed in favour of an enjoyable low priority task. Self-delusion can also creep in, when estimating how much of our time is taken up by the highest priority activities. A sales director who attended one of my seminars, for instance, was convinced he spent more than half the week motivating his sales force. Time Tracking revealed that he spent less than a day-and-a-half on this vital activity.

For these reasons, the starting point for time management is to track time by means of an accurate, written record. This is done using the charts opposite. You will find extra forms for record keeping in Appendix One.

Time Tracking

There is no need to note down everything that occupies your time; simply record each *shift in attention*, as described below.

Some people object that, since every working day is so similar, five-day Time Tracking is unnecessary. Just one day, they believe, would provide sufficient information. Another frequently voiced objection is that their job provides so much variety that even five days' tracking would fail to produce an accurate picture of how their time is spent.

Neither view is borne out by practical experience. If you believe there is little day-to-day variation in your working life, you will probably be surprised to learn just how much variety it contains. Equally, if the challenges you face seem to vary widely from one day to the next, Time Tracking will identify regular patterns of activity.

When Time Tracking, it is important to follow these six guidelines:

1 Record *each* attention shift, no matter how brief.
For example, when were you interrupted by:

- Phone calls.
- Unscheduled visitors.
- Switching to a low priority but entertaining activity in the middle of a tedious, high priority one.
- Having to attend a meeting.
- Being given work that you regard as less important than the job on which you were currently engaged.

2 Keep a track of these shifts of attention *as they occur.* Some people mistakenly believe that they will remember them accurately enough to do their Time Tracking at the end of the day. However, since memory is a poor guide to how time was spent, this never produces sufficiently accurate information.

3 On Day One complete the following columns on the chart:

- Time.
- Activity.
- Time taken.

I shall be explaining how to work out Priority Ratings in Chapter 12 and the Remarks column should be filled in after reading Chapter 13, by which time you should have completed three to five of the charts.

4 Keep your records brief, by using abbreviations:

- **T** = Telephone calls. Use an arrow pointing towards away from the T to indicate incoming and outgoing calls.
- **R** = Reading reports and other documents.
- **W** = Writing letters, memos etc.
- **D** = Dictating.
- **V** = Visitors. Tick if by appointment, or use an X to show an unscheduled visit.

You will find it easy enough to invent other abbreviations for frequent tasks and interruptions. But be sure to note these down on the top of the sheets, to avoid wasting time later trying to remember what they stand for.

5   Start Time Tracking from the moment you start work until you finally stop for the day. If you take work home, include the time spent in this way as well.

6   Keep this book beside you, making records directly on to the Time Trackers in Appendix One.   Or, if this is impracticable, photocopy the charts and carry them with you.

If you use a computer, you may prefer to set up Time Tracker on your usual spreadsheet. Some will automatically note the time of each entry and provide a total for each activity at the end of the day. You might also set up macro keys for any regular interruptions such as phone calls, to speed recording still further.

The completed Time Tracker, on the following page, shows how the charts should be kept.

Time Tracking matters

Although accurate Time Tracking is essential to managing your time efficiently, many people still fail to do so. At my workshops people offer a variety of excuses for either never starting to track, or for abandoning the attempt after only a couple of days.

● **'I was too busy . . .'**
It should take no more than five minutes daily to track your time. Indeed, if it occupies more time you are going into too much detail. Use abbreviations.

● **'It seems a waste of time . . .'**

COMPLETED DAILY TIME TRACKER

PRIORITY	TIME OF DAY	TASK	TIME TAKEN	HOW TIME MIGHT BE SAVED IN FUTURE
	8.55	Arrived - coffee	5 mins	
	9.00	Cards for 'R'	5 mins	
	9.05	Temp card for 'S'	5 mins	
	9.10	Started posters for 'M'	5 mins	
	9.15	Vv for 'R' but late so	2 mins	
		made Vv coffee		
	9.17	cont. with poster	30 mins	
	9.47	Toilet	2 mins	
	9.49	Int. by 'C'	1 min	
		about 1DPS		
	9.50	Back to poster	36 mins	
	10.26	Coffee	4 mins	
	10.30	Poster	9 mins	
	10.39	Vx for future	1	
	10.39	→ told 'M'	1 min	
	10.40	Poster	19 mins	
	10.59	Showed 'M' & 'R' poster & put it on board	16 mins	
	11.15	Upstairs & washed hands	1 min	
	11.16	Fxs for 1DP	43 mins	
	11.59	Vv for int. with 'R'	2 mins	
	12.01	Back to Fxs	8 mins	
	12.09	Wrote order form for 'G & C'	5 mins	
	12.14	Vv's CV to 'R'	4 mins	
	12.18	Printed off quote for 'C'	20 mins	
	12.38	T → Smiths	3 mins	

Far from being time wasted, the five minutes spent Time Tracking each day represent a sound investment in greater productivity. Many executives have told me they almost doubled their productivity by the end of the five-day monitoring period.

● **'I missed a day and gave up . . .'**
Then start again. Remember that since time management is really self-management, an essential component of success is being disciplined. Time Tracking helps to impose discipline on a schedule that may previously have appeared out of control.

● **'I felt guilty because it showed me how much time I was spending on enjoyable, low priority, tasks . . .'**
You need to identify exactly why deadlines are being missed. Later I will explain how you may be able to save yourself from doing tasks you either dislike, or do poorly, through effective delegation. I will also provide practical methods for getting down to high priority tasks more easily, and focusing on them to completion.

Time Track from today for at least three, and preferably five, working days.

Remember you *must* note every shift in attention between one task and the next. Even a 10-second phone call has to be recorded accurately and at the time it occurred.

3 | THE FOUR D'S OF TIME MANAGEMENT

'If I had nine hours to cut down a tree, I would spend six hours sharpening the axe.'
Abraham Lincoln

WHEN FACED with a job which is going to take up a significant amount of time, pause for a moment before getting down to it. By asking yourself four questions, you could save a considerable amount of time, effort and energy, improve production and reduce your stress. Ask yourself:

1   Does this need to be done at all?

Reflect on what would happen if it never got done. How would your goals be affected? What consequences would follow for your career, your ability to complete other tasks, to manage your department, and generally do your job? How would your company's bottom line be affected?

It may be that at this point you realise the job is a mere 'busyness' activity which can be safely dropped.

2   Do I have to do it?

You may well conclude that it is a task which can be safely delegated. But supposing it *has* to be done and only you can do it? This leads to question three:

3 Can the task be delayed?

As I explain below, there are occasions on which delay – far from being a waste of time – actually saves you time.

4 Must it be done by me, straightaway?

If the answer is a decisive 'yes', there is nothing for it but to get your shoulder to the wheel and your nose to the grindstone!

Drop it? Delegate it? Delay it? Do it? These four questions – I term them the 4-D approach to time management – take only a few moments to consider, yet save a tremendous amount of time over the course of a year. So let's look at each option in more detail.

Dropping tasks

Research suggests some time-consuming tasks are performed out of habit rather than because they are relevant to productivity, efficiency or profitability. The activity has become so routine that no one reflects why it is done or whether there might not be a more effective method of achieving the same results.

It has been found, for instance, that as much as 80 per cent of the internal paper work generated by major organisations has little or no real value. Only one in five of many thousands of reports, manuals, memos, letters, analyses and projections, which consume so much managerial time in producing, distributing, reading and filing, make a significant contribution to a company's success. The remainder merely generate 'busyness' instead of business.

The well known 80/20 rule, originally proposed by Italian economist Vilfredo Pareto, applies as much to time management as to most other aspects of business life. Pareto stated that 80 per cent of a manager's time is likely to be spent on tasks which yield just 20 per cent of his/her results, while only

20 per cent is taken up by activities responsible for 80 per cent of his/her achievements.

If correct, this means that as many as eight out of the 10 tasks which currently take up your working day are bandits intent on stealing your time. In Chapters 5-10, I shall be providing some practical ways of banishing these rapacious thieves for good.

Some idea of the savings which can be achieved by dropping inessential tasks can be gained from the chart below, based on information provided by delegates to my time and stress management workshops.

Saving Time

ACTIVITY DROPPED	*TIME SAVED PER WEEK*
Reading junk mail	30 minutes
Reading non-work-related newspapers and magazines	120 minutes
Socialising on the telephone	180 minutes
Drop-in visitors	240 minutes
Meetings	360 minutes

This is not to say that any of these tasks is, in itself, a low priority activity. It all depends on what you are trying to achieve. Spending time on non-work-related papers and magazines, for example, might be essential to satisfy a high priority goal of keeping abreast of current affairs. Similarly, relevant and well organised meetings are an essential management tool.

Knowing what to drop
The only way you ever know which activities may safely be dropped is by having clear goals, a topic we shall consider in detail in Chapter 11.

Whenever you have any say in the matter, put every task on trial by asking:

● 'Will doing this task help me achieve one of my goals?'

If the answer is 'Yes', then you need to move on to the second question:

● 'Am I the best person to do that job?'

Where the answer is clearly 'No', then – given the option of doing so – it should be dropped without delay, since every minute spent even thinking about it is a minute wasted. Unfortunately, there are bound to be occasions, perhaps many of them, when irrelevant tasks are forced on you by a superior. Under these circumstances you may be able to save time by delegating or delaying it. Both can prove significant time savers.

If you are compelled to do the work, time can still be saved by doing it as efficiently as possible.

If you decide to drop a task, drop it entirely. Doing half a job is often worse than not bothering at all. Not only does it waste time but it produces a result which satisfies nobody. An example of what I regard as a 'half dropped' job is shown in the letter reproduced below. In the course of preparation for this book, my researcher Mandy Bruce asked chief executive officers, managing directors and other busy, successful men and women about their approach to time management. Many of their suggestions are included in this book.

While I am obviously grateful to those who, despite their hectic schedules, were courteous enough to supply such information, I fully understood the reasons why others felt too pressured to help. Dropping this task was a perfectly reasonable time management option.

Cost your time

One way of deciding whether or not you should be doing a particular task is to calculate its monetary cost by completing the calculation below.

Annual salary =   £

Regular bonus or commissions received =   £

Add two per cent of net salary to cover
pensions, NI etc. =   £

Add 100 per cent of basic salary to cover overheads (office space, light, heat, phone, travel,
secretarial, administrative assistance, etc. = £ _____

Total annual cost to company = £ _____

Now divide that total by 230 (the average
number of days worked per year) = £ _____

Finally, divide the result by the average number
of hours you work each day = £ _____

Total hourly cost = £ _____

The result shows the hourly cost to your company of each
activity you undertake.

Actually this is an overestimate, since nobody can be fully
productive for every minute of every working day. But the
calculation does enable you to decide whether any task is eco-
nomically viable (of course, there may be other reasons for
wanting or needing to spend time on certain activities).

A senior manager, earning £40,000 a year plus £5,000
worth of bonuses, and working eight hours a day, costs his
company £46.75p for every hour of his time. This means that
a one-hour meeting away from the office for six such executives, which also involves two hours' preparation and travel,
costs the company £841.50p. This figure does not, of course,
take into account the cost of any subordinates involved in
preparing for or organising the meeting, nor does it include
travel costs.

Another way of looking at the equation, which applies in
many service industries, is to take not what you are paid but
what clients will be billed for your services. This can make a
startling difference to the equation. In one law firm, I know,
10 senior partners – each of whom bill their time at £400 per
hour – recently spent 90 minutes discussing whether or not
they should spend £1,200 on a new computer!

A price tag on activities
Knowing what your time is worth – and most managers
underestimate this cost – puts a price tag on activities such as

attending meetings, driving across town to meet a client, socialising over the phone, chatting with colleagues around the coffee machine, answering letters and so on.

Such knowledge is helpful in two ways:

- It enables you to be more time efficient by becoming more cost efficient. For example, through discovering new ways of completing a task more rapidly. With current levels of salaries and overheads, especially in major European, North American, and Pacific Rim cities, there is no time-wasting activity – from twiddling your thumbs to searching for a mislaid item – that does not carry a significant cost for your company.

- Being aware of that cost can also make it easier to sell the benefits of time management to superiors and colleagues. In one company where I consulted, for example, a senior executive was startled to discover that opening and reading junk mail cost his company over £7,000 a year! In another, the chairman insisted on calling frequent head office meetings which involved several managers in time-consuming travel through rush hour traffic. He was only persuaded to abandon the custom when the true cost of these usually unnecessary and unproductive gatherings was spelled out.

With the increasing sophistication of technology, such as computer networks and video conferencing, more and more companies are starting to appreciate the savings in time, stress and money to be made by avoiding frequent face-to-face meetings involving significant travelling (see Chapter 9).

If your company has yet to appreciate where such savings can be made, this simple cost analysis should help concentrate executive minds!

While reflecting on what the various tasks that take up your time cost your company, also ask yourself:

- 'Do subordinates waste my time?'

- 'Do I direct them to highest priority tasks?'
- 'Do I ever cause delays for colleagues or superiors?' (that is, by arriving late for a meeting).

Dropping a task is not the only way to save time and money. An alternative is to delegate.

Delegation

For many managers and professionals, the greatest failure of time management lies in their inability or reluctance to delegate. Research suggests that, in some companies, as much as 97 per cent of a manager's day is spent not in managing but in doing. One study found that half of all managerial time was occupied by work which would have been carried out far more efficiently by secretaries, while over 40 per cent was taken up by tasks which should have been delegated to colleagues or subordinates. As a result only 3 per cent was devoted to activities the managers were uniquely qualified to perform. Delegation enables you to spend more time on what you do well and less on what you do less well.

All successful managers recognise that effective delegation is essential for efficient time management.

Psychological barriers to delegation

Why then are so many so reluctant to delegate even the most routine tasks? The answer can usually be found in three psychological barriers:

- **Fear of surrendering their authority**

Some managers worry that, by delegating anything but the most trivial jobs, they will weaken their standing in the organisation. The truth is that, by delegating responsible tasks, and growth-enhancing tasks, subordinates become more efficient, motivated and productive. As a result, the manager who is good at delegating enjoys greater authority and status within the organisation.

● **Fear that mistakes will be made**

This usually arises from a lack of confidence in either themselves and/or their subordinates. While mistakes will always be made, this risk will be significantly reduced through appropriate delegation (see below) and careful monitoring of progress.

● **Fear of becoming invisible**

Some managers prefer to keep a tight hold on key assignments in the belief that this ensures a high profile within the organisation. However, since subordinates are therefore never groomed for promotion, the manager's own chances of advancement are diminished. There are no sufficiently experienced subordinates to take over his or her responsibilities.

Faulty delegation

None of these fears is, therefore, justified so long as delegation is performed correctly. When faulty, however, it becomes another significant cause of wasted time. Faulty delegation occurs when:

● A subordinate either does not understand and/or is incapable of carrying out the delegated task.
● Instructions are repeated many times before the task is completed correctly.
● So much time is taken that deadlines are missed.
● The work is carried out incorrectly and has to be redone – either by the subordinate or the delegating manager.
● The subordinate lacks sufficient motivation to do the work properly.

Six tasks you should never delegate

If you are a manager, there are only six tasks which ought never to be delegated:

1 **Planning a key project.**

2 **Selecting the team for that project.**

3 **Monitoring the team's efforts.**

4 **Motivating team members.**

5 **Evaluating team members.**

6 **Rewarding team members.**

Almost everything else you do is a suitable candidate for delegation.

When and what to delegate

There are four main considerations when determining which tasks to delegate. Always try to delegate:

1 When a job can be done satisfactorily by someone earning less than yourself – or less than you aspire to earn! Tasks which should normally be delegated by managers include:

- Reorganising files.
- Taking unnecessary telephone calls.
- Fitting a fuse on a desk lamp, overhead projector etc.
- Wiring a plug for the photocopier, computer, desk lamp etc.
- Typing a letter, memo, report etc.
- Taking letters to the post.

2 When you lack the necessary skill, knowledge or experience to do it efficiently. Refuse to become involved (see Chapter 5) in such tasks. Attempting to do them not only wastes considerable time but often produces a job so botched it has to be corrected by an expert – possibly at great expense and certainly at a higher cost than would have been payable in the first instance.

Repair technicians have told me that minor breakdowns on computers, faxes and photocopiers are frequently transformed into major repairs through the efforts of ham-fisted amateurs.

3 When the task is routine. They may waste your time in small amounts, five minutes here, 10 minutes there, but the total daily and weekly loss is significant. Tasks which cannot be delegated to a staff member can, thanks to technology, often be delegated to machinery. For example, a telephone which stores your frequently dialled numbers and calls them at the press of a single button. While the time saved per call is small, the total saving over a year can be considerable.

4 When the task helps subordinates to grow. These are challenges which will help your subordinates to grow by mastering new skills and gaining greater expertise. By delegating such tasks whenever possible, you not only save yourself time but enable others to enhance their skills, so taking even more of the burden off your shoulders in the months to come.

How to delegate effectively

Some managers avoid delegation because, if not done correctly, it is far quicker to do the task themselves. If you ticked the belief: 'If you want a job done well, you have to do it yourself' (see Chapter 1), the chances are your own time has been wasted in the past by faulty delegation. This can occur for three main reasons:

● Inappropriate choice of subordinate.
● Ineffective communications.
● Inadequate monitoring of outcome.

You can avoid all these pitfalls, by following two basic rules:

1 Delegate to the right person

Start by assessing the 'maturity' of your selected subordinate. Maturity in the context of delegation has nothing to do with either age or sophistication, but refers to two qualities in that individual:

● **Ability** – the skill, knowledge and experience he or she can bring to the task.

● **Motivation** – willingness to do the job to the very best of their ability.

Individuals are neither mature nor immature in a general sense, but only with regard to specific tasks. A subordinate who is mature on one task can become less mature as a result of changes in the job specification. For example, a secretary who is both skilled and highly motivated when using an electric typewriter might experience a drop in maturity (so far as typing documents is concerned) following the introduction of word processors. She, or he, may lack the experience and, perhaps, a willingness to use the new technology effectively.

Maturity can also decline in a more general way as the result of increased stress, frustrations, loss of morale, disenchantment with the work and so on, all of which reduce motivation to do the best possible job.

There are three possible levels of maturity:

● **Low Maturity** = Low ability + Low motivation

● **Medium Maturity** = Low ability + High motivation *or* High ability + Low motivation

● **High Maturity** = High motivation + High ability

The maturity of a subordinate is a crucial factor in effective delegation, so the question to ask yourself before delegating any task is: 'How mature is this individual in terms of the task I want carried out?'

Where there are several possible subordinates available to do the job, you may find it helpful to rate their ability and motivation using a simple three points scale, of Low, Medium and High. For example:

	Ability	Motivation
Mark	Medium	Low
Peter	High	Low
Mary	High	High

From this, Mary emerges as the most suitable subordinate for delegating that particular task.

Effective delegation involves providing clear, concise instructions about how, when, and where a task is to be done. It also means offering the correct amount of support and encouragement to the subordinate concerned, according to his/her needs.

If he or she lacks both skill and much motivation, you must provide detailed direction but less emotional support. An inexperienced office junior, for instance, should be clearly informed what needs to be done, when he or she has to do it and, if necessary, how to perform that task. At this low level of maturity, adopting an overly familiar or friendly attitude risks being looked on as a 'soft touch', someone whose orders can be given a low priority. This may result in the job being done poorly and delivered late, wasting large amounts of your time. And once you have earned a reputation for lacking authority, it is extremely hard to regain the respect required for successful, time-saving delegation.

Managers who alternate their delegation styles between being easy-going and 'cracking down' on subordinates create the worst of all situations, both for themselves and those working for them. Such relationships are characterised by low morale and cynical attitudes among employees. You must adopt a consistent approach to delegation at all levels of employee maturity, but especially when dealing with those who rate low on both ability and motivation.

This does *not* mean you should be off-hand or unhelpful.

Other considerations aside, to get the best out of people they must always be treated with respect and consideration. Offering a low level of 'support' simply means keeping a professional distance between you and your subordinates by emphasising that your job is to give the instructions and theirs is to obey them.

Once a subordinate has become reasonably mature, you can offer greater emotional support and encouragement, in order to enhance motivation. Now, in addition to *telling* that person what to do, you should also *sell* them on the task. Explain *why* a task needs to be done, as well as the *how* to do it.

The trap some managers fall into when delegating at this medium level of maturity is to continue to offer only directions, to a point where the subordinate feels patronised and believe that his or her abilities are insufficiently recognised. At the same time avoid providing too much support, for the reasons given above, or of assuming the subordinate to be more skilled or knowledgeable than is actually the case.

Subordinates who are both capable and well motivated need to be delegated to in a far more sophisticated manner than those with low or medium levels of motivation. Since they are both willing and able to perform the required task, the effective manager should trust them to get on with it. His or her task is to clarify, provide access to relevant data and offer emotional support both while the work is being done and on its completion. Words of encouragement and recognition for the successful accomplishment of a delegated task ensure that the subordinate remains highly motivated.

Once a subordinate matches or exceeds your level of ability and motivation, he or she must be allowed to take full responsibility for the task. Unless something is obviously going wrong, attempts on your part to interfere will, quite reasonably, be resented and result in a loss of morale and motivation.

The basic rule to follow, therefore, is that, as a subordinate's maturity increases so far as a specific task is concerned, the effective manager:

- Reduces task behaviour.
- Increases relationship behaviour.

At a high level of maturity, people see a reduction of close supervision and an increase in delegation by their manager as displaying trust and confidence. But remember that using a delegating style suited to a high level of maturity, such as participation, to a subordinate at a low level of maturity can be highly time-wasting.

2 Communicate your instructions clearly

It has been calculated that even technical workers spend up to three quarters of their day communicating with others. And in a recent survey 84 per cent of chief executives agreed communication skills were the key to promotion in their organisations. They are also essential to effective time management.

Poor communications wastes time by increasing the risk of mistakes, misjudgements and assumptions or conclusions. It lowers morale by producing frustration, resentment, bewilderment and a general sense of aimlessness within a team.

When communicating directions and instructions while delegating, go through this seven-point check list:

- **Pinpoint the task.** Establish clearly, in your own mind, the exact nature of the work being delegated. Ask: 'What is my purpose in delegating this task? What do I expect to achieve through delegation?'

In some cases several goals may be achieved, including:

- Lightening your own workload.
- Encouraging a bright employee.
- Giving a deputy useful experience.

Establish the limits of the activity being delegated. For example, are you asking a subordinate to research a report, or research and write it? Finally, make certain you fully understand what is needed here. Remember, we only understand something to the degree we are able to explain it.

● **Have you chosen an appropriate person?** Selection depends on the time, the place, the nature of the assignment and the goal you wish to accomplish.

Important considerations here are:

● **Availability** – where possible avoid subordinates with high priority tasks of their own.

● **Matching characteristics of the individual to task demands.** Does the job need to be done rapidly, with a tolerance for some minor errors, or slowly, carefully and without errors? Select a subordinate whose level of maturity matches these requirements.

● **Prepare your subordinate.** Among crucial information you need to provide are:

● **Facts about the job**. Provide a clear picture of the task to be done. Never skimp this stage, especially with a subordinate at a low to medium level of maturity. Tell him, or her, where, when and how the task is to be accomplished.

● **Relative importance of the task.** What is its priority? What other tasks may be delayed or dropped to accommodate it? Remember your subordinate will not have the same perspective on the task's importance as you do.

● **Latitude allowed.** Should it be done your way, your subordinate's way or somewhere between? How much freedom does he or she have to innovate or use initiative?

● **Never assume the other person understands until he/she has fed it back to you in your own words.** Always ask them to repeat the instructions, especially key issues such as method and deadlines. When this is being done, listen carefully. Never allow yourself to be distracted by other demands.

● **When you need to provide support as well as instructions, the key psychological aspects to concentrate on
are:**

● **Encouragement.** Make it clear you have every confidence in him or her. Be specific. Say: 'You did such a great
job on that last report, I just know you will be equally successful in meeting this challenge.'

● **Reassurance.** Make it clear that you will be available to
provide further advice or help should a problem arise. You
may also be able to identify other members of your team who
could assist. For example: 'Mary has a lot of experience using
this software package. I've talked to her, and she would be
very pleased to lend a hand if necessary.'

Where the task will involve your subordinate dealing with
new people in the company, reduce anxiety by introducing
them as part of the delegation process.

● **Enthusiasm – essential to motivation.** This powerful
force can be stimulated in a variety of ways. Which works best
depends on the psychology of that particular employee. Some
rise to a challenge: 'Frankly, this is a tough problem which
needs a determined person to crack it, but I know you will be
up to the job.'

For others, enthusiasm will be fired when allowed complete responsibility for a challenging task: 'It's your project
from start to finish, although you'll have my full backing.'

Finally, especially for subordinates at a low or medium
level of maturity, enthusiasm may be aroused by rewards, a
bonus, public credit, the chance for promotion, extra benefits and so on.

● **Monitor progress**, especially when the task is lengthy or
complex. But do not give your subordinate the impression
that you are constantly looking over their shoulder. This only
reduces motivation and creates resentment. The amount of
monitoring needed depends on the level of maturity of the
subordinate. The higher this is, the greater the resentment of

---

TIPS FROM THE TOP

Rosemary Conley

Here's how Rosemary Conley, chairman of Rosemary Conley Diet and Fitness Clubs, the UK's fastest growing franchise operation, organises her hectic schedule:

'The biggest time waster is not being organised. We can all find lots of jobs to *fill* time. But you must *use* time. Deal with important documents, enquiries and letters immediately you read them. Putting them aside to read later is a waste of time. It also means you are left with a pile of papers without being sure what's in it. This causes stress because you're not in control, and you must be in control. My diary is blocked out for weeks ahead and I try, as far as possible, to keep to that strict timetable. Everyone in my office, myself included, carries a little red book in which they record details of meetings, phone calls, and the outcome or state of play of different projects. That way we don't have an office snowed under by paper and it's easy for us to keep track of what's been going on or what's coming up in the future.'

---

a manager's 'back seat driving'. Not only does it slow them down, it also wastes your time. One method is to manage by exception. That is, only ask for reports when an exception occurs and the task is no longer being done according to the agreed schedule.

● **Beware of reverse delegation.** This occurs when a subordinate passes the task back to you in various stages, by constantly and unnecessarily seeking guidance, clarification, and assistance until you are finally doing most of the job yourself.

Provided the above steps have been followed, there should be no reason – or excuse – for reverse delegation, and all attempts on the subordinate's part to do so must be firmly resisted.

As with all skills, delegation has to be practised and polished through regular use. It is always easy to do badly and often tricky to do right. But, once mastered, you will find it one of the most powerful tools available for managing time.

Having established that a particular task must be done, and cannot be delegated, the next question to ask is whether it might be done more effectively and in less time if it was to be delayed. Although many people regard any form of delay as time-wasting, there are occasions when it can be not only the most appropriate response but the most time-saving response you can make. In Chapter 4, I shall explain when and why this happens. And I will also explain how to act when a task must be carried out – by you!

4 | THE POWER OF POSITIVE DELAY

'If you want a quick answer – it's NO!'
Buyer's slogan

DELAY,' noted Thomas Jefferson in a letter to George Washington, 'is preferable to error.' Had he written those words in the high-paced 20th century, the third American President might have added – 'and to wasting time.'

It is a fact that, while moving too slowly may lead to missed chances, moving too fast can, on occasions, result in costly and time-consuming blunders.

Procrastination

When considering the third D in the four D's of effective time management, it is important to distinguish between positive and negative delay, more usually called procrastination. This occurs whenever you defer a high priority task to concentrate on one of lower priority. For instance, rather than face up to the challenge of preparing a tough report, you may squander time by rearranging your desk top or reorganising your files. Before considering ways of using delay as a powerful time management tool, let's consider some of the reasons why people procrastinate.

1 Perfectionism procrastination

The story is told of a university history professor who constantly boasted how, one day, he would write a definitive book about his field of study, 17th-century Flemish politics. Finally tiring of this, a group of students locked him into his office, and said they would only release him when the first page of the masterpiece was complete.

Many hours later, surrounded by hundreds of sheets of discarded paper, the academic collapsed in tears over his typewriter. He had been unable to finish a single sentence, let alone a complete page, to his satisfaction. Every word he wrote struck him as falling so far short of perfection, he began all over again.

True or not, this story illustrates an attitude of mind often found among managers at all levels. By constantly striving for perfectionism they create delays for themselves, colleagues and subordinates. While it is laudable to do everything to the best of your abilities, in the real world, perfect is less good than adequate if adequate is all that achieving the goal requires.

2 Boredom procrastination

An even more common cause of negative delay is boredom. As we all know to our cost, there are certain tasks which, although essential, are less interesting than watching paint dry. Since human nature draws us towards those activities we find most rewarding and away from chores which are tedious, the consequence of being bored is often procrastination.

3 Hostility procrastination

Hostility either towards the individual who told you to undertake the task or towards your company is another common cause of negative delay. The employee who resents the fact that he or she was forced to do the job in the first place responds by staging a go slow.

4 Deadline high procrastination

Finally, there are some people who procrastinate to achieve the 'deadline high' which I described in Chapter 1. They insist their best work is done under time pressures. However, this tactic is both unhealthy and time-wasting. It increases stress levels and makes it far harder to cope with a genuine, and unavoidable, crisis. It also restricts your ability to use time as a business advantage, and creates unnecessary work for both yourself and other people:

- A document which you have read and put aside, for instance, must usually be read again before you can take action.
- Work arriving late from your department may place workers in other departments under considerable pressure.
- Files misplaced by you as a result of procrastination may have to be hunted for by somebody else.

Whatever the reason for it happens to be, procrastination is a significant cause of wasted time, and is especially damaging if you are working as part of a team.

When delay is positive

There are four occasions when delay is positive:

1 When a low priority task is delayed in favour of one with a higher priority

If uncertain how several jobs should be prioritised, use the Task Management Matrix, described in Chapter 12, to determine which you should tackle first, second, third and so on.

Try not to be sidetracked into doing lower priority activities first. Small jobs have a habit of multiplying endlessly. If you try to clear them up before embarking on urgent and important tasks, you'll never get started. Learn to say 'No' – tactfully but firmly – when others try to compel you to work on such a task.

2 When emotionally aroused

Tasks can be delayed to good effect if you feel too upset, angry, fearful or depressed to think and act clearly. In these situations, always give yourself time to calm down and collect your thoughts before taking any actions. Instead of dashing off an outraged letter to a supplier who has let you down or sending a furious fax to a colleague who behaved badly, allow some time to pass before making any response. Only after your emotional balance has been restored can you decide on the best course of action in a sensible and objective manner.

3 When you lack the information or skills to do it efficiently

If you do not have all the facts and figures needed to make a decision, or the skills required to carry out a complicated task, postpone the task until you have gathered all the relevant data or mastered the necessary skills. Never allow yourself to be pressured into judgements or responses when you are inadequately prepared.

If asked a question to which you do not know the answer, for example, it is far better to admit your lack of knowledge, then promise to find out and get back to the questioner. That way you ultimately save time and avoid a damaging error.

4 When your physical or mental state make it impossible to perform effectively

This might arise when, for example, you feel excessively fatigued or jet-lagged by a trans-Atlantic flight. Research shows that the exhausted brain is very prone to error, making mistakes and misjudgements that would never occur in a fully alert state. In Chapter 13 I provide suggestions for combating this type of stress.

Getting down to business – doing

It is at this point that some managers fall down. They know that a task is too important to drop, cannot be delegated and must not be delayed. Unfortunately, instead of getting on with the job, they fall into the trap of procrastination.

To avoid this, and carry out high priority tasks efficiently, you need to master the 10 skills shown on the Time Management Wheel of Success (opposite):

1 Self-discipline.
2 Identifying key areas for results.
3 Setting goals.
4 Controlling interruptions.
5 Planning and prioritising.
6 Avoiding procrastination.
7 Attending and/or organising effective meetings.
8 Focusing and concentration.
9 Delegation.
10 Organised work methods.

Assessing your time management skills

Rate your current level of ability (from 1 – very low; to 10 – very high) on each skill by placing an X on each of the wheel spokes, against the relevant score on pages 60–61. Then join the X's to create a graphic profile of your current strengths and weaknesses in Time Management.

Finally, total your score and write it in the first box.

The example on page 60 shows the Wheel of Success profile for a sales director called John, aged 42. He rated himself on the 10 key skills as follows:

Self-discipline 6; Identifying key areas for results 5; Setting goals 7; Controlling interruptions 3; Planning and prioritising 3; Avoiding procrastination 2; Attending and/or

THE WHEEL OF SUCCESS IN TIME MANAGEMENT
How effective are you in:-

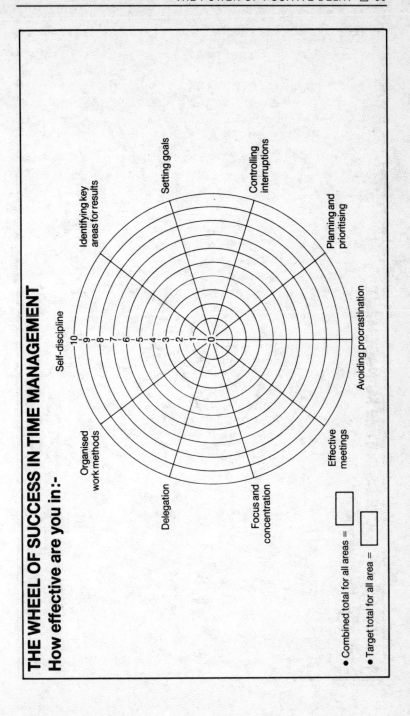

- Combined total for all areas =
- Target total for all area =

THE WHEEL OF SUCCESS IN TIME MANAGEMENT
How effective are you in:-

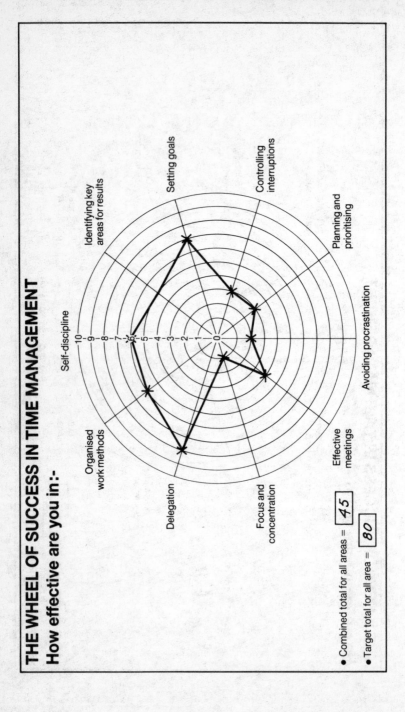

- Combined total for all areas = **45**
- Target total for all area = **80**

organising effective meetings 4; Focusing and concentration 1; Delegation 8; Organised work methods 6.

Improving your time management skills

Now examine those skills where you gave yourself a low score and consider how these might be improved by changing your present attitudes and working methods. I shall be providing practical methods to help you improve each of these skills throughout this book.

Work out a realistic target for improving any low rated skills and write this new score in the second box. Here are 10 ways to get things done:

1 Create an action list
This is probably the most widely used – and misused – tool of time management. To be effective it has to be:

● **Used daily.** Make it a part of your work routine so that it becomes automatic.

● **Selective.** Include only important, not routine, tasks. This prevents the list from becoming unwieldy and disorganised. Prioritise the tasks – in the next chapter I shall be providing a simple technique for doing this accurately.

● **Visible.** Place the action list beside you on the desk. Notes can be made in margins or between the lines, but rewrite and shorten the list if it becomes messy. This increases motivation by allowing you to monitor progress in accomplishing daily goals.

Your action list must be sufficiently flexible to cope with unexpected interruptions. An unscheduled meeting or unexpected visit from an important client, a last-minute panic at work and so on. If this causes you to fall behind, rearrange your schedule to take account of the interruption or delay. This is where having well defined priorities comes in useful.

When faced with unanticipated demands on your time it becomes far easier to decide which of your other tasks may be dropped, delayed or delegated. To qualify as a worthwhile investment of time, an activity must have been:

● **Necessary.** Avoid doing things today just because they needed to be done yesterday.

● **Appropriate.** Was it something you should have been doing or delegating?

● **Efficient.** Was there a better, faster, more time effective way of doing it?

2 Create a time map

Between you and your goal there is nearly always a limiting step – the step which determines how fast you will be able to achieve that goal. For example, if you were offered a highly paid job abroad, on condition you became fluent in the language first, then mastery of that language would be your limiting step.

Only by identifying and overcoming a limiting step can progress be made towards achieving a goal.

PERT.   One way of bringing home projects on time is to use Programme Evaluation and Review Technique (PERT). Here's how:

● Start by listing all the steps necessary to complete the project.
● Estimate time needed for each step.
● Draw a network showing relationships among the steps.

As the illustration on the opposite page shows, steps that can be completed concurrently are placed on different paths. PERT enables you to identify all the essential steps that have to be completed on time if the project is to meet its deadline.

It shows you not only the best way of proceeding from start to finish but the approximate length of each step in your journey. The example below, which is adapted from *Make Every*

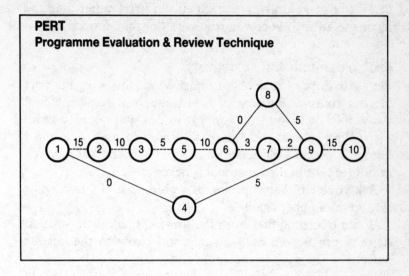

PERT
Programme Evaluation & Review Technique

Minute Count by Marion E. Hayes (Kogan Page), shows the Time Map for preparing a conference presentation:

PROGRAMME EVALUATION

STEPS TO BE TAKEN	ESTIMATE OF TIME REQUIRED
1 Research	15 hours
2 Prepare draft	10 hours
3 Check draft	5 hours
4 Prepare slides	5 hours
5 Type final draft	10 hours
6 Check proofs	3 hours
7 Type final version	2 hours
8 Prepare overheads	5 hours
9 Rehearse	15 hours
10 Deliver presentation	30 minutes

3 Get organised

Good organisation is essential for effective time management.

But never make organisation an end in itself rather than the means to an end. Focus on results rather than processes.

4 File carefully but selectively

Set aside time each week for filing. Make this a regular part of your routine. Purge your files frequently. Most material dates quickly. If you start running out of space don't add an extra filing cabinet – purge the old ones instead. Ask: Do I have to retain this material? Studies have shown that as much as 60 per cent of filed material is never looked at again.

Ask yourself: 'What problems would arise if I never saw this piece of paper again?'

When removing files from the drawer, mark their position so they can be returned quickly and easily to the correct place.

5 Stay flexible

Keep an open mind about the ways a job might be done. Avoid rigid thinking. Don't take refuge in such excuses for avoiding new working practices as, 'but we've always done it this way . . .' or 'but it wasn't invented here!' Remember what passes for common sense is often stupidity hardened into habit!

6 Take advantage of your prime time

You may have noticed that you feel more mentally and physically alert at certain times of day; for instance, first thing each morning or mid-afternoon. These are your biological prime times and, so far as is practicable, you should arrange your schedule so that the most demanding tasks can be tackled during this high performance period.

Many people find, for example, that creative work is best undertaken during the morning. Routine chores, however, may be better delayed until after lunch because many experience a natural dip in energy then.

Learning and studying are often done more efficiently mid-afternoon when studies have shown that, in many people, long term memory functions most effectively.

Because strength and stamina are greatest in the afternoon, you may find that activities requiring good co-ordination and fast reaction time become easier and more enjoyable at that time of day.

For Rosemary Conley, an early start is essential: 'In my office we all try to be there and working by eight. If, for any reason, I don't get in until nine, I feel I'm very late and I've missed much of the day.'

Sir Denys Henderson, the chairman of ICI and Zeneca, also works best at the start of the day: 'Essentially I am a morning person who starts the week on a Sunday – when I plan ahead for the next six days. Sunday is my day for serious reading and strategic thinking. I start the day early and aim to be in the office before 8 a.m. The first hour is taken up with dictation. The early start then leaves me relatively free to spend the balance of my day in making telephone calls, attending meetings, informal discussions and generally being "out and about".'

Because we are all different in the way our body clocks function, only you can know what works best for you.

As Martin Taylor, vice-chairman of the Hanson Trust, points out: 'I'm not a great believer in making strict rules, because your obligations are constantly changing as new issues arise. You have to be flexible. I think that making an early start is not necessarily essential. Some people are late starters and work on longer, and they work better that way.'

If you experience recurring dips in energy and concentration around 11 a.m. each day, the chances are that you are not eating an adequate breakfast. Include protein as well as carbohydrates in your first meal of the day; for example, by eating an egg, meat, fish, cheese, or nuts.

As the graph on p. 66 indicates, foods high in sugar produce a rapid burst of energy.

However, this quickly declines as the body over-produces insulin to deal with the sudden onrush of blood sugars. The result can be an overshoot and a sharp decrease in blood glucose around mid-morning. This condition, known as hypoglycaemia, is associated with a significant loss of

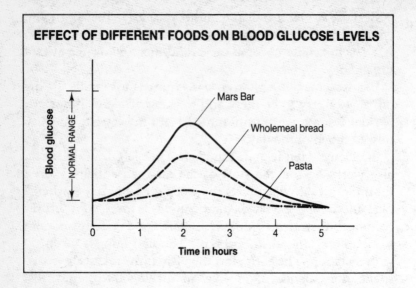

energy and concentration. Cut down on sweet snacks mid-day as well.

Avoid alcohol or a heavy meal at lunch. The former is a sedative and the latter causes blood to be diverted to the digestive system, so reducing mental and physical stamina.

Try to follow the old adage: 'Breakfast like a king, lunch like a prince, sup like a pauper.'

If you are uncertain when your prime time occurs, the best way is to monitor this over a five-day period using the charts provided in Appendix Two.

7 Do the worst job of the day first

There is a Spanish proverb which says that we should start the day by eating a live frog! If you postpone disagreeable chores until later in the day, chances are you'll brood and worry about them, so distracting yourself from the task in hand. Whenever possible, the thing you least want to do (and what could be more unpleasant than eating a live frog!) should be got out of the way first.

8 Fight fatigue by exercising at your desk

This is especially important if your work involves long periods of sitting and performing tasks such as operating a computer keyboard. Repetitive strain injury (RSI), postural pain syndromes and other work-related disorders were once believed to involve only the ligaments, tendons and muscles. It has now been established that they often have a damaging effect on nerves and blood vessels as well. Among the health problems which can result from sitting in the same position for long periods are:

- Using some muscles more than others.

- Adversely affecting the blood flow to those muscles being forced to maintain a fixed position. The supply of blood to the nerves and other structures may also be impaired.

- Bringing nerves into constant friction with structures such as bones, by distorting their pathways.

Prevent these health problems from occurring (slowing you down and undermining your health) by:

- Making certain your seat is the right height. Too high and your spine is supported only by the muscles, with a small area of the buttocks taking the body's full weight and feet offering little support. If your seat is too low, your spine will be forced to adopt a flex position, with the angles of hips and knees being too acute.

- For the same reason it is important to check that your computer keyboard is at the correct height. When seat and keyboard are properly adjusted, your posture will be such that the spine is straight and supported; your knees and hips at right angles; feet providing good support for your spine.

- Your head should be upright, rather than jutting forwards, a position often adopted by desk workers.

- Your hands should rest flat on the keyboard. Avoid a position in which your wrist is bent backwards and outwards.

- Finally, make certain the monitor is directly in front of you, to avoid constantly turning your head to left or right, and no closer than 70 cm.

At least twice an hour, stop working for 30 seconds and perform the following exercises

● Place a raised finger or pencil directly in front of you and move it slowly towards your face, keeping your eyes fixed on the object. Repeat three times.

● Place your cupped hands one over each eye. Now look up, then back to the central position. Look down, and centre the eyes again. Look left, centre your eyes. Look right, centre your eyes. Repeat whole cycle three times.

● Spend a few seconds studying some distant object – preferably the view through a window.

● Turn your head slowly first one way and then the other. Hold briefly at the end of each turn. Repeat three times.

● Draw back your head and neck, making yourself as tall as you can. Tuck in your chin, keeping it parallel to the floor. Release slightly. Your head is now in the correct position for fatigue-free posture. Relax and repeat three times.

Once an hour, stop for two minutes and perform these additional exercises

● Place your right hand on the left side of your head and use it to help bend the head to the side. Hold and relax. Do this three times.

● Hold your arms out at the side, level with your shoulders. Point your left hand thumb up and your right hand thumb down. Turn your head towards the 'thumbs down' side. Slowly turn your head towards the other hand and, as you do so, reverse the hands so you are still looking in the 'thumbs down' direction. Hold for a moment, then repeat. Do this three times.

● Interlink your fingers, palms outward. Now raise your hands slowly over your head, with elbows straight. Hold, lower your arms. Repeat three times.

- Try to touch your fingers behind your back, first over one shoulder, then the other. Keep your head and neck upright. Change arms and repeat.

- Stretch out your hands, palms and wrists together. Keeping the wrists together, move your palms as far apart as possible. Now stretch your arms without changing the position of your hands. Relax hands and arms. Repeat three times.

- Rotate both wrists, first clockwise then counter-clockwise.

- Lean forward, place your hands on your thighs, fingers pointing inward and elbows bent. Take your weight on your hands. Rest for a moment, then straighten your arms, pushing yourself upright. Hold, bend the elbows. Repeat three times.

These desk-bound exercises will help you fight the neuro-muscular fatigue that can significantly slow down mental and physical performance. They help to keep you focused and alert. But they have to be done regularly. Use a timer to warn you after each 20-minute block of time. Alternatively, where this is an option, install health-protecting software on your computer system which alerts you to take regular, programmable breaks.

9 Deadline every task
Never carry on beyond the point where the task is sufficiently well done to achieve your purpose.

Do not get bogged down in the trap of perfectionism. Often this is merely an excuse for procrastination. Keep in mind Parkinson's Law which states that 'work expands to fill the time available'.

10 Learn to focus and concentrate
Most people only work at 40 per cent of their true capacity because they have never got into the habit of being productive. Good work habits demand focus and concentration. You achieve this by having:

- Goals and objectives
- A detailed action plan
- Clear priorities
- Single-minded concentration

Whenever possible, batch work together, so that, for example, you make all your phone calls one after the other, or deal with all the mail in one session. Dodging between very different tasks is inefficient since it takes time for your brain to make the necessary adjustment from one intellectual demand to the next.

Batching similar jobs takes advantage of the learning curve. The more calls you can make in the same time frame, the more efficiently and speedily the task will be completed. Different coloured folders make it easier to batch various jobs and deal with each in turn. You might, for example, have a blue folder for calls to be answered or made, a red one for memos, a green one for letters and so on.

Procrastination, negative delay, is only one of the many barriers which can arise between you and productive work. In every office there lurk seven rapacious Time Bandits who, unless restrained, steal hours of precious time. In the following chapters we shall be identifying these thieves of time, and finding ways to keep them firmly under lock and key.

5 | BANISHING THE BUSINESS TIME BANDITS

'Doest thou love life? Then do not squander time, for that's the stuff life is made of.'
Benjamin Franklin

EACH WORKING WEEK, thousands of precious hours are plundered from companies large and small by seven ruthless Time Bandits. The daily cost of this daylight robbery runs into millions. Yet few managers even realise that they have been robbed and fewer still take positive steps to banish these rapacious villains from their premises. Yet until these business Time Bandits have been brought to book, time, effort and hard cash will continue being stolen from under your nose.

In this chapter, I shall describe ways of dealing with the first of these desperadoes: the 'Not Saying No' bandit, who gallops into your life each time you fail to refuse a time-wasting demand.

Occasions when you must say 'No'

Unless there are good reasons for agreeing, you should always refuse in the following circumstances:

FIVE OCCASIONS WHEN YOU MUST SAY 'NO'

1 **When the request is unreasonable**

2 **When the task has a lower priority**

3 **When you lack the knowledge or skills**

4 **When angry or upset**

5 **When it need not be done by you at all**

---

1 Saying 'No' to unreasonable requests

A request is unreasonable, when it

- Goes beyond your terms of employment.
- Is an intrusion into your privacy.
- Takes up your free time without justification.
- Involves saying or doing something against your best interests, principles or religious beliefs.
- Is something you simply don't want to do!

People lacking confidence often agree to unreasonable requests from fear of not being liked if they refuse. As a result, they find their time and energy being squandered on tasks of no relevance to their personal or professional goals while opening the door to further unreasonable demands. Once they have a reputation of being a 'soft touch', everybody dumps unwanted chores on their desk. Before long they are first to arrive and last to leave, with every free moment taken up by struggling to finish their own work.

Some argue that always saying 'Yes' helps them achieve the important personal and professional goals of being more popular, and advancing their career prospects by presenting themselves as enthusiastic team players.

While there is sometimes a fine dividing line between being seen as an eager beaver and a dog's body, that line does exist. Co-operating with colleagues, doing favours – especially which others will feel obliged to return – and increasing your professional experience by taking on challenges are all productive reasons for accepting extra work.

But there is nothing to be gained from getting a reputation as the department drudge. To be successful at work you need not only the respect of others but self-respect. People who meekly accede to unreasonable tasks are seldom respected by their superiors. As a result, loss of self-esteem adversely affects their prospects of promotion. Before long they look on themselves, and are seen by colleagues, as being weak, unassertive individuals whose purpose is to do the dreary donkey work.

Saying 'No' to unreasonable requests is not always easy. The longer you've allowed yourself to be dumped on the harder it will be to break free of the habit. Fortunately, the opposite is also true. The more often you refuse an unreasonable request the less guilt and/or anxiety you will feel about doing so.

When a request is clearly unreasonable, there is no need either to apologise for or to explain your refusal. Just say: 'No. I'm not able to do that.' If the other person persists, go on repeating that refusal politely and firmly, without becoming either aggressive or defensive.

Called the 'broken record' technique, this protects you against even the most tenacious time wasters because, unlike half-hearted or apologetic refusals, it offers no opportunity to undermine your position.

Where the request is on the borderline of being reasonable, some explanation – although never an apology – may be called for. If you say 'No' in a half-hearted manner, the other person will almost certainly start applying even greater pressure. Especially if, in the past, you've been too obliging and allowed others to take your ready agreement for granted.

In two of the examples of unreasonable demands described above, a half-hearted refusal might be along the lines of:

'I'm really sorry, Bob. You know I'd like to help out by completing that report for you. But I've promised my partner to leave early so we can have a game of squash.'

Half-hearted refusals are really telling the other person: 'Although I don't want to do this, I still want you to like me. You can change my mind by turning up the emotional pressure!'

Which, of course, they immediately do! One frequently used tactic is guilt: 'It's not fair. You've always helped me out in the past. I'm relying on you . . .'

Another is called the 'foot in the door' approach. Studies have shown that once we have agreed to do some small favour we are far more likely to agree to do a much larger one. This is the principle on which this tactic works. The person starts by making demands which are only a little unreasonable.

Agree, and the chances are you will also go along with the next request, which is likely to be far less reasonable and much more inconvenient.

The simple secret of saying 'No' is to mean it. Be polite, be firm, and be consistent. Do not be concerned if the other person responds by getting angry, upset, moody, or disagreeable. See these reactions for what they are – different forms of emotionally blackmail designed to persuade you to change your mind.

What about those situations in which you know the request is unreasonable yet feel compelled to agree? This most often happens when a superior insists you do something which should, in theory, be rejected. Your response then will depend on why the task is unreasonable.

If the request runs contrary to your moral or religious beliefs, invades your privacy or makes some other undue demands, then you must say 'No', even if this incurs the boss's wrath. Agree to that sort of demand and you'll become increasingly stressed and unhappy.

2 Saying 'No' when the task has a lower priority
More frequent than unjustified requests are demands which, while reasonable in themselves, have a lower priority than those on which you are currently engaged. When such a request comes from colleagues or subordinates, offer them a reasonable alternative, for which you are able to find the

time, or propose a time when it will be possible for you to undertake that task. If the request comes from a superior, then clearly you will have to voice your objections with great tact.

One strategy is to say something along these lines: 'At the moment I am giving this task priority, for the following reasons. (List the top two or three.) After that I had planned to do (list your next two priority tasks). Which of them would you like me to drop or delay in order to meet this request?'

At this point, the boss may allow you more time to complete his or her new assignment, or take responsibility for any delay in finishing a high priority task.

Other ways of saying 'Yes' to your superior but 'No' to the lower priority task are:

- Negotiate a delayed deadline. But make sure this is realistic given other commitments and the amount of work your new task will involve.

- Suggest acting as a consultant by providing the expertise while somebody else does the actual work.

- Delegate the routine parts, such as research and preparatory work, to a subordinate.

- Explain that the job lies outside your area of knowledge or expertise, then suggest somebody else better qualified to carry out the assignment (see below).

- Offer to collaborate with a colleague so that you can share the workload.

3 Saying 'No' when you lack knowledge/skills

The worst mistake you can make here is to 'have a go' at a job for which you lack the necessary qualification, just for the sake of 'showing willing'. Such requests can often be considered unreasonable. Not only will this be a waste of your own time, but it will probably waste the time of other people as well.

- 'The photocopier has gone wrong again. Could you take a look at it for me?'
- 'I can't get my car to start. Could you get it going?'
- 'I'm not sure how to run this spreadsheet on the computer. Would you give me a hand?'

Unless you are an expert on copiers, cars or computer software the most sensible thing is to refuse. While it might seem discourteous and unco-operative, a refusal is, in fact, far more reasonable than wasting everybody's time with a well-intentioned but ham-fisted intervention.

Men are especially likely to fall into this trap, since they are reluctant to admit ignorance of anything mechanical.

If you don't know – and there is no reason why you should know – refuse to be drawn into playing Boy Scout or Girl Guide.

This particular Time Bandit can also strike if you are the one with specialist knowledge and your time is wasted by well-meaning ignoramuses. Often, as well as having to sort out the original problem, you then have to deal with the consequences of their bungled 'good' deeds. On other occasions the problem could have been sorted out quickly and easily had the person concerned bothered to read the instruction book. There is no easy answer to this situation, especially when the person responsible for this bungling interference is your superior. Education and basic training offer one possible solution. So, too, does providing a simple list of things that can, and should, be checked before taking up your time. Such simple, but often overlooked, points as:

- Is the equipment plugged in?
- Is it switched on?
- Has a fuse blown?
- Is there an easily cleared paper jam in the photocopier?
- Have you removed the protective plastic slip from the toner?

Providing an easily followed flow chart, which enables even a complete novice to sort out minor problems and, more importantly, provides clear guidance on when to send for an expert, can be a great time saver.

Another approach, which I saw recently in a California computer department, uses humour to convey the message: If you don't understand don't interfere.

The department manager claimed that his notice, reproduced below, had reduced time wasted through inexpert fiddling with his technology. He said it deterred even senior management from messing about with the equipment, without upsetting anyone. We now have it posted in my company's computer department. Why not try it for yourself and see?

ACHTUNG ALLES LOOKENSPEEPERS

DAS COMPUTERMACHINE IS NICHT FUER GEFINGER-POKEN UND MITTENGRABBEN. IST EASY SCHNAPPEN DER SPRINGENWERK, BLOWENFUSEN UND POPPENCORKEN MIT SPITZENPARKEN. IST NICHT FUER GEWERKEN BEI DAS DUMPKOPFEN. DAS RUBBERNECKEN SIGHTSEEREN KEEPEN DAS COTTENPICKENEN HANS IN DAS POCKETS MUSS; RELAXEN UND WATCHEN DAS BLINKENLICHTEN.

---

4 Saying 'No' when angry or upset

Delaying an action when emotionally aroused can save considerable time.

Either explain that you feel too upset to think clearly, or simply say you need to think things over before committing yourself. If you make a decision or take an action when upset, the chances are you will regret it.

5 Saying 'No' when the task need not be done at all

Put all tasks on trial before embarking on them. Ask yourself:

• 'Does doing this bring me closer towards a goal?'

- 'If not, why do I need to spend my time on it?'
- 'If I decide to drop it, what negative consequences are likely to follow?'

Whether or not it can be dropped depends, of course, on who has made the request or given the instruction.

If it comes from a subordinate or colleague, explain why you are not going to do the task. But, before doing so, listen carefully to what is being asked. Never make assumptions about the significance of a task before learning all the facts. Only commit yourself to acceptance or refusal once you fully understand what is involved.

When the instruction comes from a superior, you may have no option but to go along with it. Bosses caught in the 'busyness' trap frequently waste hundreds, even thousands, of employee hours on costly but unproductive tasks. If he, or she, is unreasonable it may be possible to point out reasons why the task need not be done at all, or how the same results might be achieved in a more cost-effective way – perhaps through outsourcing or delegation.

Demonstrating the financial cost sometimes leads to a rethink. On other occasions there will be nothing for it but to grit your teeth and get on with the pointless chore. If such demands are a frequent occurrence, build in a margin for these time-wasting activities in your schedule.

At this point, you may like to review your Time Tracker for the past few days to see the extent to which your own schedule may have been disrupted by the first of our seven Time Bandits.

In the next chapter, I shall consider ways of banishing a second and even more merciless Time Bandit – the unscheduled visitor!

6 | DROPPING THE DROP IN CALLER

'A friend in need is a pest.'
Anonymous

A RECENT STUDY found that the average manager is interrupted every eight minutes. And, once interrupted, it takes several minutes to recover previous efficiency on the task. In other words, he or she has only been working intensively on a task for a few minutes before concentration is broken again.

The two most common causes of such interruptions are telephones (see Chapter 7) and unscheduled, 'drop in', visitors.

As you may know to your cost, some people are ruthless Time Bandits. They drop into your office or work station for no other purpose, it sometimes seems, than to chat, ask unnecessary questions, offer unwanted advice, or pass on irrelevant information or the latest grapevine gossip. Most companies, in my experience, have at least one individual who excels in the art of wasting other people's time. Not all unscheduled visitors simply want to waste your time, of course. Others compound their crime by trying to sell you something!

One widely used sales technique is to request an appointment to see the prospective customer, which concludes with the query: 'Would nine o'clock next Monday morning be convenient for you?' The sales psychology behind this tactic is to persuade you to ask yourself: 'What am I doing at 9 a.m. next Monday?' rather than the far more relevant question: 'Will the meeting help me achieve one of my goals?'

In order to defeat these drop in Bandits, you first need to understand how the layout of an office can either inhibit or encourage their unwelcome attention.

The psychology of office layouts

If you have an office to yourself, its layout will include two zones – one public and the other private.

Visitors are received in the public zone. The private zone is your personal territory.

Although an office's size and shape influence where furniture is placed, most approximate to one of the descriptions given below.

1   The desk forms a diagonal barrier across one corner of the room, facing the door.
2   The desk faces the door and creates a barrier across the width of the room.
3   The desk forms a barrier across the room, but allows for great space at one side.
4   The room is open at the door end, with the desk forming a barrier within the room.
5   The desk, pushed against one wall, no longer offers a barrier of any kind.
6   The occupant looks out of the window rather than in towards the door.

The first layout defines private and public zones most distinctly, while the last makes the least distinction between public and private zones.

Arrangements one to four, which define private and public zones most distinctly, are intended for **formal encounters**. These take place across a desk with the office's occupier remaining in his, or her, private zone while the visitor is confined to the public zone. The last two plans, which are intended for informal meetings, make the least distinction between public and private zones.

In a study by Dr Duncan Joiner of more than 130 offices, most were found to be arranged so that their occupants could see both the door and a window, while maintaining distinct public and private zones in their offices. 'Being able to see the door from one's working position implies a readiness for interaction,' comments Dr Joiner, 'and that a large proportion of the sample adopted this kind of seating position, suggests that to be able to see who is coming into the room, and to be instantly prepared for them – that is, to have one's **front** correctly displayed – is possibly more important than being able to glance out of the window.'

The word **front** means the image a worker wants to present to visitors. This is usually one designed to emphasise his, or her, status, skills and abilities.

The desire to create and establish a clear identity is so basic to human nature that some psychologists rate it as more important than an individual's desire for stimulation and security. An office and its layout are, therefore, often an extension of the occupant's personality.

The tactics of drop in visitors

In their, often successful, attempts to steal your time, Time Bandits often adopt a three-step strategy:

1 They arrive with some semi-plausible excuse for their unplanned visit:

- 'I knew you'd want to see this month's company newsletter . . .'
- 'Do you know how to operate the fax in the general office . . .'

2   They move from the public to the private zone.   By invading your personal territory it becomes far harder to get rid of them. In order to do this they have first to obtain an invitation into your private domain. One common tactic is to show you something:

- 'Take a look at the front page story of the news-letter . . .'
- 'Can you make sense of these fax instructions, because they baffle me?'

After handing the document across your desk, the visitor moves into your private zone on the pretext of pointing out something of alleged interest or confusion.

Or he or she may simply follow up their comment by immediately invading your private zone in order to hand the item to you.

3   The final manoeuvre is to sit down.   Your visitor accomplishes this either by pulling a chair into your zone, or even by sitting on the desk. Once this happens the battle is lost. You are no longer in control of events and, short of being rude and ordering him or her out, must resign yourself to having considerable amounts of time stolen by the unwanted visitor.

Dropping the drop in visitor

Here are six strategies for dealing with unscheduled visits:

1   Create physical barriers

Obstruct entry into your private zone with some small item of furniture, such as a low table or even a waste basket. Even a determined 'drop in' generally draws the line at furniture removing!

2 Guide them back into the public zone

If he or she does make it into your private zone, get them out of it as quickly as possible. One tactic is to go and fetch some document from a filing cabinet. Having done so, remain in the public zone so that your visitor has to return to continue the conversation, then gradually manoeuvre him or her out of the office.

The exact means is unimportant. All that matters is that your drop in is ejected as swiftly and decisively as possible. So long as he or she remains in your private zone, so long will you remain at a psychological disadvantage.

3 Refuse to give eye-contact

Turn your desk around so that the drop in visitor is confronted by your back, or a side view. Alternatively, when an unwelcome visitor arrives, glance up only briefly, explain that you are 'in the middle of an important piece of work', then lower your gaze again. It is very difficult to interrupt somebody if you cannot maintain eye-contact.

4 Never allow them to settle

When an unscheduled visitor comes into your office, stand up to talk. This makes it almost impossible for them to settle down for a lengthy chat.

5 Walk them out of your office again

Escort unscheduled visitors out of your office by offering to show them something outside:

'Have you seen the new poster they've hung in the general office?'

'Did you see the wonderful flower arrangement in reception?'

What you show is unimportant so long as it removes them from your office.

6 Make people sign up for your time

Your working day has two different types of time:

● **Hard time** is structured and planned in advance. It includes appointments, meetings, etc.

● **Soft time** is any of the unstructured, unscheduled periods of the day: time set aside for unexpected or unplanned events and activities.

Some managers assume only 'hard time' needs to be co-ordinated with others. They regard 'soft time' as a period when interruptions are permitted. As a result, they are often forced to respond to **pressing** rather than **priority** demands. They become slaves to their staff.

One of the challenges of effective time management is to turn all priority tasks into 'hard time', by scheduling specific areas of work, preparing a written timetable in advance and then sticking to your commitment.

When deciding priorities on a day-to-day or even hour-by-hour basis ask yourself:

● 'What is the future impact of my present actions?'

Important tasks are those which have long-term **positive** or **negative** consequences.

Knowing this helps you to distinguish between high and low priority tasks, and prevents you getting bogged down in the trivial 20 per cent of activities which can so easily come to occupy 80 per cent of our time, causing us to major in minors!

Discourage unwanted visitors by changing 'soft' into 'hard time'. Make people sign up to see you, either by calling in advance for an appointment or by writing in their names against an appointment time on your door.

Although this is not, unfortunately, an option available to every worker, if feasible, consider implementing the strategy at least one or two days a week. Alternatively, designate periods of the day, such as the time between noon and lunch, or 3 and 4 p.m., as 'hard time', when visitors can see you by appointment only. This strategy frees up blocks of time during which you can concentrate on high priority tasks in the most effective way.

When writing complex reports, for example, many managers tell me that even a brief interruption is sufficient to destroy their concentration and disturb the flow of ideas. It can then take them at least five minutes, sometimes longer, to get back into the task. In this way the unscheduled visitor, even when only able to take up a few minutes of your time, may cause much more time to be wasted.

Drop in visitors and open-plan offices

The open-plan office has the advantage of enabling teams to communicate well. When well designed, with adequate sound baffles and noisy equipment sufficiently insulated, the benefits may even outweigh the disadvantages. No matter how well laid out, however, open-plan offices are probably responsible for more wasted time than any other single innovation.

Not only do many people find it harder to concentrate, they become far more vulnerable to unscheduled visitors. Because it is intended to allow free access to employees, the design mitigates in favour of time-wasting visitors. I know of no perfect strategies for repelling these space invaders. But among tactics which managers have told me worked well for them are:

● **DIY traffic lights.** One woman manager constructed a set of toy traffic lights from a sheet of cardboard and some coloured markers. A simple shutter allowed her to cover or uncover each of the 'lights' in turn. Then she told her staff: 'If the red light is uncovered, only interrupt me when the building is on fire. When I uncover the amber, you are welcome to approach with important, high priority queries. If the green is showing, you are free to come with any problems.' She found this light-hearted approach was generally well received.

● **Ear muffs.** A male manager, finding it impossible to concentrate because of all the noise in his open-plan office, hit on the idea of buying ear muffs. And instead of choosing the discreet little wax plugs which sit invisibly inside the ears, he chose a pair of large, ostentatious Mickey Mouse muffs. These not only cut down unwanted sounds, but also made it abundantly clear to colleagues that he was not to be disturbed!

● **Planning and co-operation.** Because everybody is likely to be equally inconvenienced by interruptions, it's a good idea to hold occasional meetings of all those working in the area. Problems can then be identified and ways of improving the environment discussed.

TIPS FROM THE TOP

Stephen Rubin, chairman, Pentland Group

'It is essential to have a good secretary who filters out time-wasting calls, and only puts through those which are important and at a time when they do not disturb other meetings. Unless you take this precaution, you will find that you can never have an uninterrupted meeting.'

Once again you may find it useful at this point to look through your Time Tracker notes to see how many interruptions were caused, and time consumed, by the drop in Bandit. Use the most appropriate techniques described above to help cut down these losses.

7 | HOW NOT TO GET HUNG UP ON PHONE CALLS

'The great advantage it possesses over every other form of electrical apparatus consists in the fact that it requires no skill to operate the instrument.'
From a prospectus for Alexander Graham Bell's Electric Telephone Company, 25 March 1878

PICTURE THE SCENE. One of your colleagues, driven to despair by his workload, clambers on to a tenth floor window ledge and threatens to jump. You begin coaxing him to safety. Then, just as he is on the point of climbing back inside, the telephone rings. Would you answer it? Hardly.

Yet you may behave no less illogically every time you interrupt a high priority task for what often turns out to be a lower priority phone call.

Screening, referring and delegating calls

Telephones must, of course, be answered promptly and courteously if your company is to be regarded as polite and efficient by customers and suppliers. But this need not mean *you* must always be the one to answer it.

Screening, referring and delegating calls can save you significant amounts of time. So, too, will limiting the conversation to the business in hand, since research suggests a majority of calls go on far longer than is necessary to satisfy their purpose.

As a result, a piece of equipment which should be one of the greatest time savers ever invented is all too often transformed into a predatory Time Bandit.

Potent time saver

Used correctly, of course, the telephone is a potent time saver:

- You can communicate more rapidly and efficiently by phone or fax than in any other way.

- It enables you to contact people you might otherwise have to travel to see.

- Mistakes and misunderstandings can be cleared up instantly.

- The telephone is your company's front line ambassador for the majority of those doing, or seeking to do, business with you.

TIPS FROM THE TOP

Geoff Shingles, chairman, Digital

'My greatest time saver is having a computer terminal and facsimile at my home as well as my office. Using these I am able to make an early start on those jobs which I normally do by myself. I can do this at times when I would, otherwise, be sitting in traffic jams and I can then go to the office or appointments outside peak traffic times. My life no longer revolves around the physical location called "my office" thanks to a set of tools which act as vital life support aids. This has relieved me of an enormous amount of stress and pressure.'

Poor telephone technique

But beware. The telephone is a two-edged weapon capable of losing you both time and business as swiftly and surely as it can gain them.

I have calculated that as much as 40 per cent of wasted time in some offices is due to poor telephone technique. If that sounds improbable consider this: a recent survey by the research company Teleconomy found that of 3,000 calls made to 300 different companies, over a third of the calls rang more than eight times before being picked up, yet only one per cent received an apology for being kept waiting.

For the lucky ones who actually made it through the first hurdle of the switchboard and got put through to the right extension, further time wasting occurred. Callers were left holding on while the right person was tracked down; very few were given an instant answer to their query, and 44 per cent who asked to be called back by someone who would provide answers to their query never received the return call.

If you think that never happens at your office, try an experiment. Call from an outside line with a tricky request. Use a name which is difficult to pronounce and remember, then ask to speak to someone who can help solve your problem. You may be disagreeably surprised to find how much of a customer's time your staff are wasting.

Remember that 95 per cent of most companies' daily contacts come via the telephone, and the way they are treated has a dramatic impact on their desire to do business with you, whether for the first time or as established callers.

Twenty ways to save time on the telephone

Contrary to the proud boast of Bell's Electric Telephone Company, using the telephone correctly demands considerable experience and skill. Here are 20 ways to prevent phone bandits from stealing your time.

1 Limit social conversation. Avoid time-wasting and irrelevant discussions. Without seeming discourteous, come swiftly to the point if you have initiated the call, and prevent somebody who called you from straying too far off the track.

2 Provide short answers to questions. Do not feel tempted to elaborate needlessly. Say what you have to say and then end the call as soon as its purpose has been achieved.

3 Make sure that the key part of your message is clearly remembered, by using what psychologists call the 'primacy and recency' effects. This simply means we recall most easily and accurately those things heard first and last. This explains the advice often given to public speakers, that they should: 'Tell 'em what you are going to tell 'em. Tell 'em. Tell 'em what you've just told 'em.'

When giving complicated information or instructions over the phone, start with a brief summary of the message, follow that by repeating it in greater detail, and conclude by briefly reviewing the key points.

4 Delegate the taking of calls whenever possible and appropriate.

5 To avoid being disturbed by calls, do work demanding intense concentration earlier in the day – either from home or by coming into the office before everybody else. Where possible, use a room without a phone for work demanding intense concentration.

6 Refuse to take any calls between certain times.
During this period all calls are either delegated or held.

7 Anxiety aroused by difficult calls can waste time in several ways. You may delay making such a call, even though the matter is urgent and must be resolved promptly. When calling you may find it hard to think clearly and objectively. Your memory for facts and figures is poor, forcing you to consult notes, records, memos and so on, adding further delay.

Physical tension also makes it far harder to express yourself clearly. You stammer and stutter, hesitate and prevaricate. If your anxiety is sufficiently high, you may end the call before your purpose has been achieved. This, of course, only wastes further time since you have to make the call again. Research shows that anxiety-induced tension in the vocal cords makes men sound irritable and inflexible, while women are judged to be emotional and irrational. Finally, anxiety prevents you from listening carefully enough to prevent time-wasting errors and misunderstandings.

By banishing needless tension through a rapid relaxation exercise immediately before placing a stressful call, most of these difficulties can be avoided. Here's how to unwind quickly and discreetly while still seated at your desk:

- Deliberately tighten your muscles. Clench your fists, curl your toes, flatten your stomach and take a deep breath. Hold all this tension for a slow count to five.

- Now exhale slowly and let those muscles go limp. Drop your shoulders, unclench your fists, uncurl your toes, relax your stomach and rest back in the chair.

- Take another deep breath and hold this for five seconds. As you breathe out, make certain your teeth are unclenched.

- Breathe quietly for a further five seconds and, as you do so, feel relaxation flowing through your body.

- Finally, soothe jangled nerves by picturing yourself lying on the golden sand of a sun-warmed beach by a clear blue ocean. Hold this image for a few moments.

You are now mentally and physically prepared to lift the receiver and make that difficult call.

When you are through to the person concerned, go directly to the main point. If your message is complicated, jot down the key issues before dialling and use your notes to guide you through the conversation.

8 Encourage co-operation by using the phrase: 'Will that be all right?' immediately after suggesting some course of action. A study by the Equitable Life Assurance Society has clearly demonstrated that using this simple phrase significantly improved the chances of reaching agreement. They found this simple question:

- Encourages a positive response from the person you are calling, and does so in a friendly manner.

- Brings the other person back into the conversation at any point where you either seek feedback or need to reinforce a key part of your message.

- Subtly compels him or her to agree with your proposition by responding 'Yes, that will be all right.' This answer is the most likely one, since people will nearly always do what is easiest. It takes a very stubborn individual to reply negatively to such a cordial enquiry. The more 'Yeses' you can extract, the more likely it is you will achieve your overall goal. If you have asked 'Will that be all right?' a couple of times already, the other person has developed the mind set of saying 'Yes'. This increases the likelihood of them agreeing to more demanding requests.

9 Taking the initiative and making calls places you at a psychological advantage in three important ways:

- *You* have decided to take up the other person's time and he or she has agreed to allow you to do so. In accepting your call, therefore, the other person has allowed himself/herself to be, at least temporarily, dominated. It also means you can call at a time which suits your schedule, instead of being interrupted in a higher priority task.

- Because you can choose how the conversation starts, you have a better chance of directing it along the lines most advantageous to you. This can save time by preventing needless diversion and back-tracking. It's the difference between driving a car and being driven.

- Finally, whoever initiates a call is in the stronger position to end it without causing offence, so saving further valuable time.

10   Before dialling, always have a clear idea of what you hope to achieve by making that call.   Ask yourself, 'What is my purpose in phoning this person?' If you are trying to fix an appointment, in a situation where refusal is anticipated, have several possible times and dates in mind.

As I explained above, asking: 'Would 10 a.m. on Friday the 23rd be convenient?' focuses the other person's mind on whether he or she is free to see you, rather than whether he or she really wants to see you!

11   Always start your conversation with 'Good morning . . .' or 'Good afternoon . . .'   This gives the other person time to tune in to your voice, and switch concentration from their previous task to that of dealing with your call.

It also makes it more likely that your name, which should be given in full, and the name of the person you are calling – if speaking to a receptionist or secretary – will be understood. This saves having to repeat the information.

12   Calling at an inappropriate moment is a major time waster.   The person you need to talk with may be out of the office, in a meeting, with clients or unable to take the call for some other reason. The worst time to call is first thing in the morning, when the other person is catching up on mail, dictating letters, planning the morning calls and generally getting the day under way. Last thing at night is equally unhelpful since people, not surprisingly, resent being delayed on their way out of the office. Always ask: 'Is this a good time to talk briefly, or should I call you back?'

13   Telephoning while standing literally heightens your sense of authority while sharpening your mind.   When we are upright, our mind and body become more alert and attentive. This makes it easier to understand complex ideas and take in difficult facts the first time around, without wasting time by asking for them to be repeated.

14   Listening is a skill which must be learned, practised, and perfected before it can be used successfully. One source of errors is that our brain understands speech faster than most people talk. During normal conversation people speak at around 120 words per minute, yet your brain is able to make sense of speech delivered at 500 words per minute.

To add to the risk of becoming distracted, normal conversations are full of repetition – the same idea may be restated several times or repeated in a number of slightly different ways. Then there are sounds and phrases such as 'umm . . . er . . . mmmm', and phrases like, 'you see . . .' 'I mean . . .', and 'You know . . .'.

Slow speech, repetition, redundancy and meaningless sounds can quickly drive all but the most skilled phone user to distraction. Yet unless you are able to concentrate, much time will be wasted through mistakes and misunderstandings. Key information will be misheard or forgotten, making it necessary to take up time by calling back. Avoid this trap by prioritising your calls. When talking to that person over the phone is more urgent and important than anything else you have to do, give the call your undivided attention.

If the call has a lower priority than the task on which you are currently engaged, ask to return it at a mutually convenient time. And then be sure to do so!

15   Always listen positively when phoning.   This involves not only listening to what is said, but paying attention to those words left unspoken.

There are three types of positive listening:

● **Diagnostic.**   You listen in the same way a good doctor listens to his or her patients before making a diagnosis. Remain non-judgemental because any comments, especially criticisms, may well inhibit the other person's flow of ideas and increase his or her reluctance to address the deeper issues, thus making it harder to get to the root of their needs.

● **Reflective.** Involves paraphrasing and repeating what the other person has said. This saves time by preventing you acting on a false assumption, since you have confirmed what has been said.

Repeating comments also helps impress them on your memory, making it much less likely that important points, ideas, facts or figures will be forgotten.

● **Empathic.** Means putting yourself in the other's situation. Seeing things from his or her viewpoint helps you appreciate the pressures of time, money or other resources which the other person is working under.

Empathic listening also allows you to identify that individual's favoured style of communication, based on one of the personality profiles described below.

16 Disraeli once remarked that there was 'no index of character so sure as the voice'. By gaining insights into the way the other person thinks, you can match your conversational style to their needs and expectations more easily. This saves time by soothing the flow of communication, and reducing the likelihood of misunderstandings. As you listen, remain relaxed and allow an impression of the speaker to form slowly in your mind. These unforced impressions are often remarkably accurate:

● **A fast speaking rate** – provided the content makes good sense – is correlated with above average intelligence. Someone who talks quickly usually thinks quickly. So you can probably speed up the rate at which information is communicated without risk of confusion.

● **Hesitations, stammering, pauses** often betray areas of anxiety or indecision. In this case, slow down when providing key facts and figures. And always check they are fully understood – remember that anxiety significantly impairs comprehension and concentration. This saves you time by avoiding the necessity to respond to calls for clarification. If the facts are complicated, then it's worth while confirming them by fax immediately after the call.

17 People like to be communicated with in various ways. If you match the content of your call to these personality needs, you will save time by getting your message across promptly and clearly.

● **Commanders.** Some people use the language of achievement. They speak of 'setting goals', 'working towards objectives', 'planning ahead', 'making progress', and 'moving forward'. Their tone is brisk, business-like and purposeful. They will finish your sentence for you, impatiently, and end the call abruptly once they've achieved their purpose.

When making or taking calls to this personality type, be brisk, direct and to the point, since they heartily dislike time wasters. Have a clear idea of what you want from the call before dialling. Stress how your ideas can help them attain goals or make more efficient use of their time. Your tone must sound brisk and confident.

● **Comforters.** People who come into this category talk more about intuition and emotions. They use phrases such as 'My feeling is . . .', 'My hunch is . . .', 'I sense that . . .', 'My gut reaction is . . .'. They tend to talk more slowly and quietly, listening carefully to what you have to say and paying close attention to your views. They expect even business calls to have a sociable element. So be prepared to devote a little more time than usual to chatting in a friendly fashion. Ask about their health, how their children are doing in school, discuss the weather. Listen to their ideas or problems. Your tone should be warm and empathic.

● **Dynamos.** Use words and phrases which convey energy and enthusiasm. They'll tell you '. . . That sounds great', 'This is a really exciting project', 'I'm thrilled by your ideas', 'You will love this'. Dynamos speak quickly, urgently, and excitedly, with ideas often tumbling over one another, such is their speed of delivery.

They enjoy variety in their conversations, and quickly become bored, so don't be afraid to introduce several different topics, or to jump from one idea to the next. Speak in a lively, enthusiastic manner which conveys a sense of urgency and excitement.

● **Planners.** For this personality type, facts and figures are of the greatest importance. They use phrases like 'Consider the facts', 'Speaking objectively,' 'Logic suggests', 'The way I figure it', and 'I think we must'. They speak slowly and carefully, reflecting on their words and instantly correcting any mistakes you may make. As with Commanders, keep social chat to a minimum and provide relevant facts and figures precisely. If you don't know an answer, say so honestly rather than taking a guess. Say you will find out and phone back. Speak firmly, clearly and unemotionally. Confirm the main points of your discussion with a faxed summary.

18   A universal rule of human relationships is, other things being equal, that we like best those who seem to like us best. By communicating a positive, sincere interest in the other person, you can develop that sense of friendship on which consumer loyalty is based. As you glean information through chatting, make a note of it, either using a written telephone log or directly on to a computer (bear in mind the Data Protection Act).

When calling a company or individual for the first time, enter as many details as possible on the Time Log on page 98.

Photocopy these sheets and keep them close to hand, in a folder or file. Alternatively, you may prefer to copy out the headings on to index cards. When you have a number, sort them into alphabetical order. A Telephone Log saves you time in three ways:

● Provides immediate access to all the key information needed, so saving you from having to track it down in several files, records etc.

● Allows you to speak directly to the person who can answer your queries or initiate the actions you require.

● Prevents time-wasting errors when a number is misdialled or misrouted.

As a bonus, it also helps you develop a close relationship with key suppliers and buyers.

Essential details include the name and address of the company, their phone number and the extension of the person you want to call, together with his, or her, name – the correct pronunciation if this is unusual or difficult – and their position in the company. Before phoning, check all the details needed to handle that call efficiently.

Knowing exactly who you need to talk to is the fastest way of getting through the outer defence of receptionists and secretaries which most senior executives use to protect their time and privacy. Keep the relevant Telephone Log sheet by you as you make the call, and complete additional entries immediately after putting down the phone. Include personal details discovered during the conversation, such as the names and

---

TELEPHONE LOG

Name: Company:

Position:

Phone: (Office)   (Ext)

(Home)

(Mobile)

(E-Mail)

Fax:

Date first phoned:

Personal Details:

Remarks:

ages of children, hobbies, interests, likes and dislikes, and so on. Used judiciously, personal information of this kind significantly increases the speed with which you can develop a close working relationship.

19 Get the best out of answering machines

If you run, or do business with, small businesses, the chances are you'll find yourself talking to, or trying to persuade others to talk to, an answering machine. In theory these devices should be great time savers, by ensuring that important calls are never lost. In practice, answering machines can turn out to be yet another telephone Time Bandit.

There are five main fears which make it difficult for some people to get the best out of answering machines:

● **Technophobia.** Some people are irrationally afraid of technology. For them, communicating with an electronic gadget ranges from disagreeable to downright terrifying. You can often identify technophobes by the messages left on your machine: 'Hello, Oh God don't tell me I'm talking to a machine . . . Oh . . . Oh . . . call me back!' Since they seldom leave a name or phone number, their call is rarely returned – thus wasting time and deepening their loathing of the machine.

● **Help by:** Planning your message carefully. If caught unawares by a machine, ring off, work out what you want to say – maybe writing down key points – then re-dial. Be sure to give your name and phone number, briefly state the purpose of your call and include time and date of the message. When preparing an out-going message (OGM) for your own answering machine, make certain it is clear yet sufficiently comprehensive to ensure you get all the information needed.

If, for instance, your machine only allows a brief message to be left, then make this clear on your OGM. Your voice should sound warm, affable and welcoming. Check for user friendliness by calling your own line from another phone. Ask yourself whether, if you heard that message, you'd be most likely to leave a message or hastily replace the handset.

● **Sounding inarticulate.** Many people take time to get into the swing of a conversation. They have to warm themselves up with some casual chit-chat before getting around to the main purpose of their call. The answering machine makes them fearful because it inhibits this preliminary warm-up.

Help by: Keeping the message short and always including any action you want taken, such as being called back.

● **Running out of time.** Knowing that a tape is unwinding worries some people. They are afraid they will run out of time before saying all they need and want to say. This causes them to forget key points in their message.

Hence the need to plan, and perhaps even write down, what you want to say – at least until you have become accustomed to using the answering machine.

Help by: Using the suggestions above. In addition, forget that you are speaking to a machine and imagine the person you wanted to talk to is listening at the other end. (Sometimes they will be!)

● **Being recorded.** Some callers are fearful of their hesitations and errors being recorded.

Help by: Giving yourself positive feedback after leaving a message. Notice all the good things which you did. If anything about the way you dealt with the answering machine was unsatisfactory in your view, then identify the problem and work out a better way of responding next time around. If you own an answering machine, analyse the way other people leave messages.

● **Being misunderstood.** Some people dislike acting on messages left on answering machines, from a fear of misunderstanding your instructions. If even slightly uncertain about a message, they may waste time by waiting until they can talk face-to-face.

Help by: Leaving short, concise messages. Spell any tricky words, such as names and addresses, using Alpha/Bravo code where appropriate. For instance, to give the Post Code AC20 0BY it may be better to say A for Alpha, C for Charlie 20, O for Oscar, B for Bravo, Y for Yankee. Repeat numbers, dates, times etc. Speak slowly and clearly. If the message is a complicated one, try to leave a number where you can be called back to clarify the message.

20 Ending a call efficiently is no less important than starting one correctly

Chatter on for too long and you risk confusing, boring or irritating the other person. For a satisfactory conclusion:

● **Be polite.** When dealing with a relative stranger use their name in your final sentence. If there are some facts you particularly want remembered, repeat them immediately prior to saying goodbye. The way memory works means we recall best the things heard first and last in a conversation.

● **Be firm.** Avoid being diverted into an irrelevant discussion. If you find this hard to do, have a few plausible excuses such as, 'Sorry, I'm wanted on the other phone,' as a standby tactic. Usually, however, if your tone is positive the other person will get the message. Having said farewell . . .

● **Be gone.** Replace the receiver and start thinking about the next call you want to make.

Saving other people's time on the telephone

So far I have looked at ways of saving time when making calls. But help others save time, too, by observing the following rules for incoming calls:

1 Your telephone should never be allowed to ring more than three times (12 seconds) before being answered. If it does you'll lose customers who can't be bothered to hang on for your convenience, and you will create a negative image among those patient enough to wait.

2   Everybody in the office should take responsibility for answering a ringing phone.   This means training them in good telephone technique and providing them with sufficient knowledge about the organisation to deal with enquiries efficiently and speedily. They must know who should be contacted for any particular caller, and how to put them through to the correct extension.

3   There should be a specific procedure for the taking and passing on of messages.

- Staff should know what details are required if the person is to be called back.

- Return numbers should always be taken, even if the caller assures you it is known to the person to whom he wishes to speak.

- The telephone should always be answered as follows:
  'Good morning/afternoon/evening, this is (give number or name of company or both), Mary Smith (name of person answering here), how can I help you?'

The structure of this response is important. As I explained above, starting with a 'Good morning', etc., allows the other person to direct their attention to your call. While waiting for the receiver to be picked up, even if it has been answered within the required 12 seconds, the caller's mind tends to wander. As a result he or she will usually fail to attend to the first second or so of the response. If you immediately answer with the number or company name, the caller may not be fully attentive and could get confused or ask you to repeat it. Either wastes time – yours and theirs – and is easily avoided. Identifying the company and/or number is clearly important to reassure the caller he/she has dialled correctly or, if it is a wrong number, to establish this fact promptly in order not to waste time.

Giving the person your name establishes a positive relationship right from the start. It makes you personally, and your organisation, sound welcoming and friendly.

4 Never answer the telephone while eating or drinking, or in the middle of a conversation with someone in the office. Either ask someone else to take the call or stop what you are doing and give your whole attention to the call.

5 Never put one hand over the phone to speak to someone nearby. It makes your organisation sound small and unprofessional.

6 If you promise to phone back, then do so. Few things are more calculated to annoy prospective customers than messages which remain unanswered.

7 If you don't know the answer to a question or problem, then admit as much and promise to return the call with the correct information either personally or by contacting the appropriate employee within your organisation.

8 Check the key points of your conversation using Reflective Listening. This prevents unnecessary and possibly costly blunders.

9 Always thank the caller for taking the trouble to ring.

10 Allow callers to hang up before you do. Replacing the receiver while they are still on the line means ending the call on an unfriendly note.

Now go through your Time Tracker, noting the number of occasions on which you were interrupted by phone calls which had a lower priority than the task on which you were engaged. Consider how, by using some of the telephone savers described above, you might have prevented this particular Bandit from stealing so much of your time.

8 | BEATING THE WAITING BANDIT

'Things may come to those who wait, but only the things left by those who hustle.'
Abraham Lincoln

The extent to which other people are able to waste your time by keeping you waiting depends on several factors, not all of which lie within your control. Taking up the time of others is sometimes used as a weapon during corporate power plays. The higher up the pecking order a person is, the greater their ability to waste other people's time. At the top, you can make appointments to suit your convenience rather than theirs and, when necessary, keep them waiting almost endlessly for the privilege of seeing you.

Power play – the waiting game

Some powerful executives deliberately keep staff waiting as a means of emphasising their status. The late Robert Maxwell, for example, was notorious for summoning senior executives to a meeting and then forcing them to kick their heels outside his office, sometimes for a whole day at a time, before finally declining to see them at all.

'Your position in the waiting hierarchy often determines your importance,' comments Robert Levine, professor of psychology at California State University, Fresno. 'The longer the line, the more important the person becomes. The value of financial consultants, attorneys or performers is enhanced by the simple fact that they are booked up well in advance . . . the least accessible are sometimes elevated to saviour-like dimensions.'

An unwritten rule in American universities say students must wait 10 minutes for an assistant lecturer, 20 minutes for an assistant professor and 30 minutes for a full professor. When put to the test, in a study by psychologists James Halpern and Kathryn Isaacs, this rule was found to be widely followed.

Being kept waiting for more than 15 minutes beyond your appointed time, without reasonable explanation or apology, may, therefore, be a power play on the part of the person you are expecting to meet. There are, of course, exceptions to this rule, but research suggests it is a widely adopted tactic designed to put the visitor at a disadvantage, placing him or her in the role of a supplicant rather than an equal.

A sales person, for instance, who waits more than 15 minutes for an important buyer is being told, in none too subtle a fashion: 'You need me far more than I need you! You have less status and importance in any forthcoming negotiations than I do, and should therefore be willing to accept my terms.' If the sales person allows his or her confidence and esteem to be damaged by this tactic, as is the intention, the subsequent deal may be far more favourable to the buyer than would otherwise be the case.

In any encounter there are only three responses open to you:

1 To Dominate the other person (people)
2 To Submit to the other person (people)
3 To Co-operate with the other person (people)

● **The dominant encounter.** A dominant encounter is often called a zero-sum game. This is an expression derived from 'winner takes all' games, such as poker, where one player's gain is another's loss. Zero-sum games are characterised by the presence of winners and losers.

● **The submissive encounter.**   During such meetings the other person's gain is your **apparent** loss. I emphasise **apparent** since the only justified reason for voluntarily submitting to the will of another in a business encounter is with the expectation of enjoying greater rewards at a later date.

In the Chinese ancient manual of war, the *Bing Fa*, generals are advised to 'tempt the enemy with small gains', a philosophy now frequently, and successfully, followed by Pacific Rim negotiators in their dealings with the West. The strategy can be likened to that of a chess player who allows minor pieces to be taken by his or her opponent, while laying a subtle trap leading to checkmate. You might also act submissively from a desire to appease a high status individual with power to determine your future.

● **The co-operative encounter.**   Co-operative or non-zero sum games are those in which all players gain something from the exchange and walk away from the negotiations feeling satisfied. But it must be noted that even during a co-operative game you may sometimes need to dominate the proceedings, while accepting a more submissive role on other occasions. In other words, the encounter should be approached with a flexible attitude and a readiness to tempt your opponent with small gains.

It is important to bear these points in mind when deciding how best to deal with unnecessary and unreasonable delays.

How to deal with power play delays

Your best course of action if kept waiting, without explanation or apology, for more than 15 minutes beyond a scheduled appointment time depends on three factors:

- Your status relative to the other person.
- The reason for wanting the meeting.
- The overall goal you seek to accomplish.

If you want to remain on an equal footing with the other person, and are in a position to do so, my advice is to leave at the end of 15 minutes unless there has been an adequate explanation for the delay. After a quarter of an hour, any unexplained – or unconvincingly explained – postponement of a confirmed meeting is almost certainly a power play.

The other person is trying to shake your confidence and diminish your status through deliberate delay. Instead of wasting further time, explain to the receptionist or secretary that you are unable to wait any longer and will phone to reschedule the appointment. Ask for this message to be passed on to the person concerned, and make certain this is done. At this point one of three things will happen:

1 The person you are meeting will agree to see you right away. This is the best outcome, since it neutralises any edge he or she might otherwise have gained from the tactic of deliberately making you wait.

2 A reasonable explanation for the delay may be forthcoming, together with an assurance that you will not be kept waiting much longer. Accept this at face value and agree to wait a few minutes longer. Once again, such a response will remove any psychological benefits the other person might otherwise have enjoyed.

3 He or she may make no response. If this happens, your bluff is probably being called. You must now make good on your ultimatum and walk out. You must do so even if the apparent losses from such a walkout seem to outweigh the benefits of kicking your heels for a little longer. If you continue to wait before being finally ushered in to your postponed meeting, the psychological advantage will have passed to the other person. Even if he or she apologises for the delay with apparent sincerity, you will have placed yourself in the submissive role before you have even started to negotiate. This works against you in the discussions which follow.

There will, of course, be many occasions when such a response is not available to you. For instance, where the other person is of much higher status or you need him or her more than he or she needs you. In this instance, all you can do is recognise that a power play is being used against you and that the other person feels a need to dominate the appointment.

Rather than feeling resentment at such discourteous treatment, merely acknowledge the reality of the situation – you genuinely are the supplicant in this instance – and do not allow it to affect your confidence and self-esteem. Keep busy and, when finally summoned to the meeting, keep him or her waiting for a few minutes while concluding your call, finishing a calculation or filing away a report.

Not only does this send a small, but perhaps significant, signal to the other person but also allows you to feel more in control of events, a psychological plus on entering to go into an important negotiation. This approach should enable you to transform a meeting in which you have been placed in a dominated role to one which more rapidly moves towards co-operation.

SIX WAYS TO AVOID WASTING TIME BY WAITING

1 Always confirm your appointment
2 Organise to minimise travel time
3 Never arrive more than five minutes before your appointment
4 Allow for a margin of error
5 Make your sure your arrival is announced
6 Keep yourself busy

---

1 Always confirm your appointment beforehand, especially when this involves a journey across town. Some sales people are reluctant to do this out of fear that the prospect will cancel on them. The best way to avoid this risk is by calling the secretary or receptionist and saying: 'This is .... I have an appointment with X at 10.30 a.m. (or whatever the time is). Just to let you know I am on my way.' Even if 'X' has forgotten the appointment, such an approach will usually persuade him or her to make time to see you.

Another useful tactic is to confirm an appointment by fax or letter immediately after it has been made. But confirmation on the day is especially important where an appointment has been made more than a week in advance.

2 Organise your appointments to minimise travel time. Strange as it may seem, some otherwise well organised business people are quite willing to criss-cross congested cities to get from one appointment to the next.

This can be the result of confusing being 'busy' with doing 'business', a mistake I have mentioned previously.

So long as the wheels are turning, they feel that something is being accomplished. On occasions, there may be no choice but to set up meetings in this way. Often, however, some careful forward planning can greatly reduce time spent travelling, while making it less likely that an unexpected delay on the journey will possibly cause you to miss your time slot.

3 Although you should arrive in the vicinity of the meeting place in plenty of time, do not enter reception until five minutes before your appointment. This is usually sufficient time to give your name and details of the appointment to a receptionist or security guard, or to find your own way to the relevant office.

If you arrive much earlier, you will be sending all the wrong signals. The message of very early arrival is that you are:

● **Not especially busy** and – by inference – not especially successful and/or

● **Over-eager to do the deal**, see that person or conduct whatever other transaction the appointment was made for.

Turning up only moments before your appointment is also risky, since any delay at reception may make you late. In some circumstances this could well get the meeting off to a bad start.

Either way, too early or only just in time, you are immediately placed at a psychological disadvantage.

4   Reduce stress, where possible, by giving yourself a margin for error.   Instead of saying: 'I'll see you at 3.30 p.m.' say: 'I'll see you around 3.30 p.m.' This enables you to turn up between five and 10 minutes earlier or later without causing offence. Your ability to make such a general appointment does, of course, depend on the nature of your business and relationship with the other person. But in these days of ever increasing traffic congestion and unavoidable delays, many people are prepared to offer such latitude. Incidentally, a mobile phone can also be a great stress reducer, enabling you to phone ahead and either apologise for a delay or even reschedule the appointment, should some major problem occur.

5   On arrival, clearly announce your name and that of the person you have come to see.   Then wait at reception until the person you are expecting to see is contacted. In a busy, and/or poorly organised reception, it is not unknown for your contact to remain ignorant of your presence in the building.

6   While waiting, always keep busy.   Do not sit staring into space or reading a newspaper. Not only does this squander precious 'dead time' which can be put to productive purposes but also sends out all the wrong messages to the other party. It suggests you have nothing better to do with your time than hang around somebody else's reception, diminishing your status in their eyes. Dictate letters, work on calculations, read reports, memos or cuttings from your folders. Ask the receptionist if you can use the phone – the request is rarely refused. That way you not only put the time to good use, but cut your own overheads while doing so!

9 | DEFEATING THE MEETING BANDIT

'Are you lonely? Hate having to make decisions? THEN HOLD A MEETING. You get to see other people, off-load decisions, feel important and impress your colleagues. Meetings – The Practical Alternative to Work. Hold One Today.'
Anonymous

ALWAYS THINK LONG AND HARD about whether a meeting is really needed at all. Huge amounts of precious time could be saved in most companies by banishing the Time Bandit of formal meetings to the wilderness.

Whenever possible, make routine decisions informally. Hold brief meetings in the corridor, around the coffee machine, in the car park even. Experience suggests that formal meetings are usually only necessary if making decisions on which the company's future depends.

It has been estimated that in the UK alone, more than four million hours, or some 450 years, are spent attending meetings each and every working day. While some meetings are essential and unavoidable, others are black holes into which time vanishes without trace. And the one thing virtually all have in common is that they could be conducted faster and far more efficiently. While a proportion of the thousands of people attending those meetings will be making constructive suggestions, listening intelligently, reaching sensible decisions and helping to solve pressing problems, many more will be indulging in self-aggrandisement, enjoying the sound of their own voices, playing office politics, staring out of the window, doodling, picking their nails and longing for coffee to arrive.

How not to hold meetings

There are six ways in which meetings can turn into costly exercises in time wasting.

1 'What are we doing here?' Lack of preparation results in a meeting lacking any clear overall plan or goal. People attend without really knowing why or what is expected of them.

2 'If it's Tuesday we must have a meeting.' Routine meetings held out of habit rather than for any clear-cut purpose are among the biggest Time Bandits in business. They frequently reflect the vague belief that it's a good idea to 'get the team together', without offering any specific agenda. Avoid this trap by asking:

● 'What goal (corporate or individual) will this investment of time (individual and collective) help achieve?'

3 'Does anybody know what we're talking about?' Breakdowns in communications can occur before, during and after meetings. Misunderstandings beforehand result in people arriving poorly prepared. A failure to clarify issues during the meeting leads to confusion, unnecessary discussion, missed opportunities and frustration. Inadequate communication of the ideas and decisions arising from that meeting prevents necessary actions being taken or agreed changes put into practice.

4 'Let's do something daring!' It is widely believed that individuals take more risks than groups. In fact, the opposite is true. This is due to a phenomenon called the 'risky shift', first identified by psychologist J.A. Stoner during the 1960s. He demonstrated that meetings are more likely to propose high risk policies and take daring decisions than the same individuals would do on their own. A number of explanations have been put forward for the 'risky shift', including diffusion of responsibility, which enables everybody present to blame anybody else for any mistakes made and the fact that a risk-taking, charismatic leader can often sway more cautious group members to his or her viewpoint.

Paradoxically, another characteristic of some groups is that they are unable to come to any conclusion, and talk endlessly around the subject. People attending meetings tend to confuse discussing with decision making, a particular failing of bureaucrats unconcerned by commercial realities.

5 'Better defer to the experts.' Meetings can waste time and money through a faulty use of resources. It happens when unsupported assumptions on the part of those attending the meeting are allowed to pass unchallenged. This is especially likely when lay members are reluctant to challenge the opinion of experts.

In *Effective Meetings* Phil and Jane Hodgson recount how, as part of Ronald Reagan's ill-conceived Star Wars initiative, scientists mounted a mirror on a satellite designed to reflect back a laser fired from Earth. The radar responsible for aligning this mirror was designed to lock on to a 13,000 feet high mountain in Hawaii.

Unfortunately, it had been calibrated to search for a mountain 13,000 *kilometres* in height, and, failing to locate one on Earth, locked on to the Moon instead. As a result, the mirror faced into space rather than earthwards, and the experiment was a multi-million dollar fiasco! Mistakes like this, which are far from uncommon, arise when people attending meetings are misled by unchallenged assumptions. The underlying cause of such confusion is often a failure to prepare adequately, which allows the opinions of the most dominant or most vehement to triumph.

'When in doubt do nothing.' Because changes are hard for people to accept, many decisions taken at meetings are never implemented. After a flurry of interest immediately following a ground-breaking meeting, the status quo is quickly restored by those with a vested interest in everything continuing as before.

How to save time when organising meetings

Because those organising meetings have the greater power and responsibility for ensuring everyone's time is spent wisely, let's start by looking at 12 proven ways for making every meeting both productive and time effective.

1. Set clear goals
2. Provide everyone with a written agenda
3. Keep the number present to a minimum
4. Avoid on-the-hour starts
5. For brief agendas keep everyone standing
6. Use the 'talking ball' technique
7. Check consensus with straw polls
8. Try newmawashi
9. Arouse interest via careful planning
10. Keep everybody focused
11. Prevent one-to-one discussions
12. End with a call to action

1 Set a clear goal for your meetings

Ask: 'What purpose will be served by this meeting?' Is it to:

- Make a decision?
- Analyse or solve a problem?
- Provide the group with new information?
- Gather data about the state of a particular project?

Be clear in your own mind exactly what outcome you are aiming to achieve. Write this as a single line mission statement and place it in clear view of all those attending – use a flip-chart, placed within easy reach.

2 Provide everyone with a written agenda

Every meeting, no matter how brief, should have a written agenda. This should be circulated as far in advance of the meeting as is realistically possible, to allow those attending time in which to prepare. Without a prioritised agenda, meetings are very likely to degenerate into general discussions instead of staying focused on the key issues.

Ask yourself how you want those attending to emerge from the meeting. What changes in their attitudes or behaviours are you looking for? Explain your agenda at the start of the meeting, then move directly to the main purpose.

3 Keep the number present to a minimum

Invite only those who need to be there. Calculate the cost of the meeting – based on the wages and overheads of all those present – then write this up on the flip-chart below your mission statement.

4 Avoid on-the-hour starts

Studies have shown that people are more likely to be punctual when attending meetings that are held off the hour. More people arrive late for a meeting scheduled to start at 10 a.m., for example, than for one which begins at 10.10 a.m. Why this should be is unclear, but companies which have switched to 'off hour' starting times report better punctuality. You should also set a finishing time for the meeting, and stick to it.

5 If the agenda is brief, keep everyone standing

This is now widely adopted for short meetings. All chairs are removed from the room, and those attending remain standing throughout.

This tactic offers two benefits:

- People are more alert when standing than when seated and so less likely to miss important points.
- Nobody wants needlessly to prolong the meeting, so the agenda can be worked through far faster and more efficiently.

6 Use the 'talking ball' technique

Pioneered by Texas Instruments, this involves passing a rubber ball around the group, only the person actually holding it being allowed to speak. This saves time by preventing the speaker being needlessly interrupted.

7 Take regular straw polls to check consensus

People sometimes talk more to air their views than resolve conflicts. Prevent this by taking informal polls from time to time to assess consensus. If there is general agreement on a course of action, it can be put to the meeting instantly for a formal vote, instead of wasting time on unnecessary debate.

8 Try the Japanese technique of Nemawashi

In Japan, it is common to hold meetings to prepare for meetings. While this may appear to encourage the exponential growth of meetings, Nemawashi can be a major time saver.

It involves bringing together small groups of specialists for brief discussions prior to one or two of them attending the meeting. For example, a group of engineers might meet the day before a major project meeting, to resolve any outstanding technical issues and agree on a collective approach.

Although this technique arose in a culture which places far more emphasis on consensus than is common among Western business people, the idea is a sound one which has now been widely implemented. It saves time by allowing the delegates from specialist, or special interest, groups to make immediate decisions instead of insisting on referring the matter back.

9 Arouse interest through careful planning

Exert a positive influence over the attitudes and expectations of those attending by:

- Obliging everyone to prepare for the meeting. You might, for instance, announce, well in advance, that each person will have to make a five-minute presentation on the biggest problem he or she has encountered since the last meeting.

- During the meeting, select speakers randomly.

- Make everyone present feel their involvement is valued and that important information can be gained from the session.

10 Keep everybody focused

One way of doing this is to calculate the cost of the meeting (by applying the formula given in Chapter 3 to all attending) and write this in large numbers on a flip-chart. When they realise what each of their irrelevances costs, even the most determined side-tracker tends to watch his or her tongue!

11 Prevent one-to-one discussions

If two participants lock horns and begin to discuss an issue between them, excluding the rest of the group, immediately reschedule the issue as a meeting between just those two protagonists. Then firmly call their attention back to the purpose of the present meeting.

12 End with a call to action

Encourage all those attending to take some clear action as a result of the meeting, by making it clear you intend to follow up on what was agreed. Then do so!

Network meeting details

Keep a master meeting schedule on the department computer so everyone can call it up. This makes it easier and faster to schedule meetings while keeping the whole office informed.

Organising larger meetings

When more than a dozen or so people are involved, follow the points described above but in addition prevent boredom and lapses in concentration by:

- Putting variety into the voices of the speakers. Go from a male to a female speaker and then back again.

- Varying the format, pace and style. Keep the audience on their toes by never allowing the meeting to become predictable.

- Using team presentations and panel discussions, rather than allowing one or two speakers to drone on for hours.

- Balancing topics on the agenda. Avoid, for instance, allowing one motivational speaker to follow another, or two speakers in turn to present hard-to-digest statistics.

- Sandwiching topics non-specialists find less interesting, such as financial statements, between items of more general appeal.

- Breaking large groups into smaller teams to encourage participation by everyone.

- If visual aids are employed, vary them rather than presenting entirely with the aid of video, OHP fiches or 35 mm slides.

- The use of colour on slides and overheads will enhance interest and lead to greater attention.

Saving time when attending meetings

If attending somebody else's meeting, follow these 10 rules:

1 Be prompt. Do not waste other people's time by arriving late.

2 Be prepared. Make sure you have all the relevant documents and have fully briefed yourself on what will be discussed.

3 Be there only if you need to be. If you have any choice in the matter, put the meeting on trial just as you would any other time-consuming activity.
- Why are you attending the meeting?
- What do you expect to get from it that will help you to achieve a goal?
- What are the costs and benefits?

4 Be involved. Participate in the discussions. Do not sit quietly and allow everybody else to do the talking.

5 Be attentive. Much time is wasted in meetings because people just do not bother to listen carefully to what is said. As a result, they raise points which have already been debated and ask questions to which answers have already been provided. Use the positive listening techniques described in Chapter 7.

6 Be relevant. Make sure your remarks, comments and suggestions genuinely address the central issues facing the meeting, and are not merely an excuse to demonstrate your own wit or wisdom.

7 Be brief. Say what you want to say and then stop. Avoid rambling on.

8 Be courteous. Do not interrupt another speaker, however much you may disagree with the point he or she is making. Allow them to finish before expressing your views.

9 Be focused: issues not individuals. Much time is wasted in meetings when one person attacks another, rather than raising doubts about the point that the speaker has just made.

Personal attacks are disruptive and unproductive. They waste time by compelling others to defend themselves and/or launch a counter offensive. And by raising the emotional temperature of the meeting, they distract others from thinking clearly about the major issues.

10 Be action oriented – follow up. Where a decision has been taken which affects you, always act on it.

Alternative forms of meetings

There is an increasing trend towards organising meetings – especially those held in-house – at which people participate via video screens or computers rather than face-to-face. For example, one major company in this field, Skills Dynamics of Canada, a part of IBM, for example, now has a thousand regular business users.

During such meetings, those attending present their views over a computer network and need not be in the same room, or even in the same country. Computer conferencing is suitable for groups of up to 35 and – apart from cutting down on the need to travel – offers a number of time-saving and other benefits:

- There is no risk of the meeting grinding to a halt because one bore insists on dominating the proceedings. All attending can contribute on equal terms.

- Anonymity makes it easier for delegates to express views

which are different or unorthodox, and honestly to express likes and dislikes.

● When the purpose of the meeting is to innovate, electronic brainstorming has been shown to unlock greater originality and creativity.

● By reducing the emotional content of discussions, computer-based meetings offer a low-key method of discussing contentious topics, such as ranking employees for promotion.

● The system provides instant feedback, to ensure comments remain relevant, and immediate minutes at the end of the meeting.

Neither computer- nor video-conferences are suitable for one-on-one discussions; negotiations with groups, such as unions, who distrust management technology; or when experts are presenting their views.

An increasing number of major companies share similar views about improving corporate efficiency through replacing many of their in-house meetings with well-organised video-conferences.

Saving time when travelling

As we have just observed, travelling to meetings – or, indeed, the actual journey time involved in any form of business travel – can be a great time waster. So, before setting out on any business related trip, pause and ask yourself: 'Is my journey really necessary?'

Calculate the cost of making such a journey (using the same formula given in Chapter 3) and consider whether the same result might not be achieved faster and far more cost effectively over the telephone, by fax, E-Mail, or video-conferencing. When several people will have to travel a considerable distance to attend a meeting, for example, this last option can save a tremendous amount of time and money.

TIPS FROM THE TOP

Sir Peter Walters

One strong advocate of a more extensive use of video-conferencing between major corporate centres is Sir Peter Walters, chairman, Midland Bank, Blue Circle and Smith Kline Beecham.

'My own interest in this stems from the early 1980s, when I noticed that the head of BP's North Sea exploration activity, which was located in Aberdeen, had to make some 90 visits to London each year. Not only was this physically exhausting and disrupting to his family life, it was also a terrible waste of time. This caused us to embark on an extensive set of video-conferencing facilities which, as well as London and Aberdeen, connected London to our US head office in Cleveland, with later links to Houston and Alaska. Not only were significant cost-savings involved, but a well-planned two hour video-conference released management from two or three days away from the office and spared them inevitable jet-lag. But there are, naturally, times when you must have face-to-face personal contact, especially with outsiders such as customers or suppliers.'

Using travelling time productively

If a journey is unavoidable, travel by the fastest and most comfortable route the budget will allow, and use that time productively. While driving or being driven, for example, listen to teaching and training cassettes which will help you improve your professional skills or acquire new ones. A number of companies produce recorded book summaries and extracts from major business publications.

There are also language and motivational cassettes covering a wide range of topics.

Train versus car

Whenever convenient, travel by train instead of car. It is usually a more relaxing and cost effective method of transport, since, as well as reading documents, you can also write or use a lap-top computer.

TIPS FROM THE TOP

Sir Colin Marshall, chairman, British Airways

'Invest in a driver. While the idea of being chauffeured around may strike some people as extravagant, it allows you to do a great deal of work in what would otherwise be dead time. I read mail, and other papers, as well as making telephone calls. These distinct business benefits far outweigh the cost. Finally, go by Concorde for transatlantic travel. I know this comes into the category of "he would say that, wouldn't he", but it is a valid suggestion. Concorde is the only way to buy time. Supersonic travel from London to New York effectively stretches the day by six hours and 10 minutes.'

Planes take the strain

Flying, too, should be used for productive work, whether working or taking the time to think through strategy or a presentation. One study showed that an hour in first class can be equal to three in the office. If you are going to work, improve productivity by choosing a seat next to a window. That way you will avoid being disturbed by fellow passengers pushing past you on their way to the galley or lavatory. You should also choose a seat away from the galley or lavatory, since these are the noisiest and most disrupting of offices.

Bulkhead seats, although they sometimes offer slightly more leg room, are also better avoided. Taking a seat one row back ensures you will keep your briefcase with you throughout the flight. Safety regulations require cabin staff to stow the carry-on luggage of passengers in bulkhead seats, which means your case may be in an overhead locker several rows from where you are seated.

If you intend using a lap-top computer, check with the airline first since some forbid their use in flight. This can prove extremely frustrating for a business passenger who meant to put in several hours of work on a computer during the journey. Although a majority of airlines allow lap-tops to be used, except during take-off and landing, I have been refused permission by, among others, Air Maroc and Iberia. Equally, I have never been refused by BA, Virgin or any of the American carriers.

TIPS FROM THE TOP

Martin Taylor, vice-chairman, the Hanson Trust

'These days, a great deal of any manager's time is devoted to an enormous amount of necessary reading, and you can use travelling time in cars and planes to do that. Of course, portable phones have proved extremely useful in business, especially in cutting out what was previously dead time in driving from one place to another. But, having said that, you can also use that "dead" time effectively as a welcome opportunity to pause and think about other things, so that when you reach your destination you are fresh for the next meeting.'

---

10 | SAVING TIME WHEN READING AND WRITING

'The Lord's prayer is only 56 words long; Lincoln's Gettysburg Address is 268 words long; the Declaration of Independence is 1,322; and the Federal government's cabbage code, which regulates the sale of cabbages, is 26,911 words long.'

Complaint of US Congressman

READING AND WRITING reports, memos, letters, books, journals, papers and other business documents already takes up a significant amount of the average manager's working day.

The rapid growth in bureaucratic demands, government rules and regulations, and the pressing need to update professional or business knowledge suggests the situation can only get worse. Unless we take steps to outmanoeuvre him, this last of our seven Time Bandits could prove the most rapacious of them all.

Improving your reading skills

Fortunately, we have ample scope for saving time by improving the primary school-taught skills of reading and writing.

Research suggests that, with an average reading speed of

200 words per minute against a possible 1,000 words per minute, even well-educated men and women read five times more slowly than is necessary. Were they to read at their true potential speed, the time taken to read a book, for example, might be cut from five hours to 60 minutes or less.

The blame for our time-wasting habits can be laid fairly and squarely on how we were taught to read in junior school. During those early lessons children are, typically, required to stand up and read aloud to teacher and class. If words are missed, they are told to go back over them. As a result, many adults needlessly slow down their reading speed by:

- Silently turning words into sounds inside their heads.
- Reading every word.

These techniques are neither necessary nor desirable. The printed word can be interpreted with perfect accuracy without first transforming printed symbols into unvoiced sounds, and the amount of redundancy found in virtually all types of material allows a considerable amount of skipping without any loss of comprehension.

Myths about rapid reading

Myth: 'Rapid reading is hard to master and I just don't have the time.'

Reality: Any literate adult can double or treble their reading speed with little effort or expenditure of time.

Myth: 'Rapid reading involves serious loss of comprehension.'

Woody Allen jokes that, after taking a rapid-reading course, he read *War and Peace* in four minutes. 'It's about Russia,' he says. Many people who read for business rather than pleasure worry that that jibe has more than a grain of truth in it. They are concerned that, by reading faster, they will miss or misunderstand vital facts, figures, ideas and concepts. Because their early learning involved reading 'every word', they feel guilty and anxious about missing anything out, however irrelevant to their needs.

Reality: Research has found little relationship between reading rate and understanding. Some people read rapidly and with excellent comprehension, while others read painfully slowly and have only a poor understanding of the material.

Myth: 'Rapid reading involves training your eyes to take in more information – such as whole paragraphs – at a single glance.'

Reality: Although this method was once taught by some rapid-reading courses, this is a waste of effort. What slows reading is not taking in the information via the eyes but processing it in the brain. Now for the good news.

Rapid reading is easy

There is nothing difficult or special about achieving reading speeds of between 800 and 1,000 words per minute for a wide range of business related texts. While it is true that you may need to slow the rate when dealing with highly technical or complex information, for most managers this comprises only a small part of their essential weekly reading. The secret of rapid reading is to adopt the right approach.

At the risk of seeming to digress, imagine – for instance – you wanted to explore an uncharted desert island in the hope of locating minerals or the best site for a new hotel, or a coconut plantation.

One approach would be to land on the beach and set off purposefully in some direction, hacking your way through the undergrowth and making a note of all the features you encountered on the way.

Having arrived at the other side, you could repeat the process, criss-crossing the island until you had charted every square yard. While methodical, this approach is also time-consuming and may provide more information than you actually need to achieve your purpose. In short, you'd be wasting time by using the wrong approach.

A majority of people adopt a similar strategy when reading. They start at the first page, reading every word, in every line, on every page, until they eventually arrive at the last paragraph.

An alternative, and far more efficient, way of surveying the island would be by air. You would start at a sufficiently high altitude to gain an overview of the whole landmass, then gradually fly lower and lower to examine finer details.

Having pinpointed the areas of greater interest, you could then land and explore on foot, this time confining your attention to those locations most relevant to your goals. Efficient reading involves adopting a similar – global – strategy.

The global approach to reading

Before reading any text, ask yourself three crucial questions:

- 'What is my purpose in reading this material?'
- 'Which of my goals will be satisfied by reading it?'
- 'Is this text the best way of satisfying that goal?'

If there is no good reason for reading it, then save time by dropping that task (see Chapter 3).

Should you decide the material is worth investigating further, adopt what I term the global approach to efficient reading. Skim rapidly over the pages to get a general idea of the book's structure and content – chapter headings, section headings within the chapters, charts, illustrations and captions – the equivalent of a first sweep at high altitude. During this initial overview, locate items of special significance in achieving your reading purpose.

Just as a person exploring a desert island would be searching out very different landmarks if his purpose was, say, prospecting for oil rather than looking for the ideal place to site a hotel, it is your reading purpose to determine which of the ideas and concepts, facts and figures presented in the book will be most relevant.

Once these key landmarks have been identified, the next stage is to organise your thoughts by creating a mental map which will guide your more detailed exploration of the text. You should also reflect once again on whether the material needs to be read at all. Now that you have a better idea of what this 'island' has to offer, are you certain it can satisfy your reading purpose? Or would it be more sensible to select another 'island' which promises better returns on your time?

Reading to suit your needs

On the assumption that you do decide to read on, the next step is to arrange the text to suit your reading purpose. Do this by re-ordering the chapters or sections in such a way that they best meet your specific needs.

While reading a technical book, for example, you might find that reading Chapters 5, 9 and 3, in that order, will provide all the information needed. These chapters can then be explored in depth, using a combination of the three methods of reading described below.

The final stage is to label the sections, paragraphs, sentences or words of greatest relevance by underlining or highlighting them, adding notes and comments in the margin. By actively working with text in this way you not only develop a clearer understanding of the material but also significantly enhance recall of key information.

Changing gear as you read

While reading, constantly vary your pace – just as you would change gear while driving – to take account of the varying demands you need to make on the text. There are three reading speeds:

● **Skimming – fast.** This is the fastest way of reading, at speeds of 800-plus words per minute. You read at this pace to find short answers to questions starting with who, what, when or where:

- Who was involved?
- What was happening?
- When did it happen?
- Where did it happen?

By keeping these questions uppermost in your mind as you rapidly skim the text, you will find the answers jump right off the page at you.

- **Scanning – medium speed.** This involves moving at a slightly slower pace through the text, achieving speeds of between 400 and 800 words per minute. It enables you to search for answers to more longer and more complex questions starting with why and how:

- Why did some event happen?
- How did it happen?

- **Studying – slow down.** Finally, there is critical reading – where the material is explored in detail for deeper meanings. But, just as only a small area of the island needed to be surveyed on foot, so too, is there only a limited amount of text that demands this most time-consuming form of reading.

Use a pacer card when skimming or scanning

Guide your eyes swiftly down the page while skimming or scanning by using a sheet of plain card (or your hand) as a pacer. Here's how:

- Place the card, or your hand, flat on the page above a line of print. By covering what has been read as you move it down the page you prevent time-wasting backtracking.

- Move the card (or your hand) down the page. Keep your gaze fixed on the line directly beneath it.

- Adjust your reading speed by making the card, or hand, move slower or faster down the page, while making certain your eyes keep pace with the guide.

- Do not try to read an entire line at once. Instead identify whatever words you are able to in each line as the card/hand 'pushes' your eyes down the page.

Practise this technique in training sessions during which you move your guide faster than in normal reading. This will help you to feel relaxed about reading at high speeds. Set yourself realistic goals for increasing your reading speed.

To do this, you must first establish your current speed, as follows.

How to measure your current reading speed

Take some unfamiliar material, typical of the texts you normally or frequently read in the course of work, and time how far you can read – at a level of comprehension which meets your needs – in exactly one minute.

- Calculate the number of words read as follows:

1 Count the total number of words in 10 consecutive lines. For example, this might be 140 words.

2 Divide the total by 10 to obtain the average number of words per line. Using the given example, you would have 14 words per line.

3 Count the number of lines you read in one minute.

4 Multiply by the average number of words per line to measure your reading speed.

If the material is also available in a word-processing package, use the word count facility to provide an immediate, and more accurate, check.

Reading the six most common types of business material

Having looked at general methods of increasing reading speed, let's consider the most efficient way to read the six most common types of business material. The basic approach is to identify where to look for the information you require.

This enables your eyes to go straight to the correct location instead of travelling all over the text in a haphazard search.

1 How to read newspapers and magazines more rapidly

With a magazine, always begin by looking through the table of contents and identify articles of relevance to your reading purpose. Do not waste time browsing but go directly to the significant material; resist the temptation to be distracted by interesting but irrelevant articles.

A good way of handling this type of material is to cut out relevant articles, then file them into different folders. Depending on the nature of your business, you might have one for features about your competitors, another for articles on the latest technology or marketing techniques, a third for management techniques and a fourth for personal growth/health improvement features.

By gathering material on the same topic, from various sources, you get a more informed and rounded view of the subject. Carry one or two clippings folders around with you, and read them during 'dead times', such as when waiting for an appointment or travelling by plane and train.

Newspaper and magazines contain three types of material:

● **Feature articles.** The purpose of these is to inform and entertain. They provide background material and typically use examples and anecdotes to illustrate key points. They also normally start with an example of what the writer has in mind.

● Scan the article, focusing your efforts on the middle and final portions of text, which normally describe the main ideas and key facts. These are frequently identified by bullets – as I have done in this and other sections of the book.

● The first and last paragraphs can normally be skipped without loss of comprehension, because they provide solely illustrative anecdotes or examples.

● **Opinion articles.** These are designed to make you think in a particular way or take some specific action.

● Often you need only read the first paragraphs, which typically contain these ideas or actions, and the final paragraph which usually summarises the key ideas.

● The paragraphs between, which typically provide supporting reasons and examples, may not be necessary for your comprehension and can be safely ignored.

● **News articles.** Typically, these contain more hard information and far fewer examples, anecdotes or background than feature material does.

● Since they usually prioritise information, starting with what the editor regards as the most important item and concluding with the least significant, read the first and the last paragraphs before skimming the intervening material.

● In a news magazine, charts and graphs may be used to summarise key facts, figures and concepts. Examine these first to gain an overview of the content.

2 How to read office memos more rapidly

If you examine your company memos, you will probably find they have a similar structure: with key information such as source, subject and intent (that is, information or action requested) located in the same place on each.

- Save time by immediately directing your gaze to these areas of the memo. There is seldom any need to read the whole thing.

- While reading a pile of memos, sort them according to priority. For example, place high priority memos to the left and low priority memos to the right.

3 How to read company reports more rapidly

- Start by obtaining an overview, so as to gain an idea of both the individual parts and how they are organised into a whole.

- Skim through the pages and notice how the report has been structured. Even where a table of contents has been provided, you should still skim and scan to see how the report has been put together and locate any subheadings omitted from the contents list.

- Now recheck your reading purpose. What can you do with the information contained in this report? How will knowing the content help you achieve a goal?

- Create your own contents list on a sheet of scrap paper. Note down key ideas and facts, together with their page number.

- Rank contents in order of your own personal priority. This may well be different from the printed contents, which reflect the author's priorities.

- Finally, skim, scan or study relevant sections – always keeping your reading purpose firmly in mind.

4 How to read technical manuals more rapidly

- Identify the manual's purpose. This is normally given towards the front. In what and to what circumstances does it apply? Who is affected by the information it contains?

Which of your goals will be satisfied by reading it?

- Review the material and get an idea of overall organisation. How has the manual been structured? Are there charts, illustrations etc. which could aid your understanding? How complex is the material?

- Understand the logic of how the information has been structured, that is, by order, functions, circumstances, personal groupings and so on.

- Skim and scan the pages, dipping in and out of different parts of the manual.

- Notice whether or not there are specific items you must be aware of and keep in mind to understand the text, for example acronyms, technical terms, company codes, definitions and so on. If any are unfamiliar, make notes on a separate sheet of paper and look them up before starting to read.

5 How to read technical books, reports and papers more rapidly

Seven factors make these among the most time-consuming of all the material you have to read:

- Their information content is high and there are few redundancies. This leads to a rapid onset of mental overload.

- Significant levels of knowledge about the subject are normally assumed.

- Concepts can be complex and require careful thought.

- Specialised terms are used which demand precise interpretation.

- The style is often verbose and the material poorly organised.

- Print size may be small and information contained in long sentences and wearying paragraphs.

- Diagrams, illustrations, charts and formulae are often poorly located in relation to explanatory text.

How to read them. As before, start by defining your reading purpose. Ask yourself:

- 'What do I need/want to get out of this text?'

- 'What level of comprehension is necessary for that purpose to be satisfied?'

- 'Is reading this book/report the best way to satisfy my reading purpose?'

- 'Is it pitched at somebody with my level of knowledge?'

- 'What authority does the author bring to the report?'

- 'Is he or she a recognised authority in this particular area? Are the writer's credentials sufficiently impressive to make my investment of time worth while?'

- 'How recent is the material?' Bear in mind that in many fast developing fields, a report may be, to a greater or lesser extent, out of date almost as soon as it has been published.

If you decide it should or must be read, use the global technique:

- **Begin by obtaining an overview of the article.** How has it been structured? Does it include descriptions, procedures, case histories, problems and ways of solving them? Are key concepts explained or is an understanding of them assumed?

What help is provided for the reader? Is there, for instance, a glossary of technical terms and acronyms? Is there a table of contents, and if so, is this detailed or superficial? If the latter, you may find it helpful to create your own table of contents.

- Identify key concept words and phrases which carry the author's main ideas. If any are unfamiliar, clarify your understanding of each before reading further. Such keys are usually located in predictable parts of the report or book, such as the glossary or index, or the table of contents – especially when detailed. This table of contents also provides a general idea of the way in which the text has been organised.

Make a point, too, of reading the introduction or preface. Many readers skip this in the mistaken belief that to do so speeds their progress through the book. However, since many writers state the major purpose of their book or the main premise of the report in the introduction, it should always be read. Introductions often provide a summary of the text, and may also explain key concepts.

Then read the first and last paragraphs in every chapter or report section. Do not try to speed read anything at this stage. Instead dip in and out of the text. When you have done so, reflect on what you have read. Write down any questions which this initial survey raises in your mind. Mentally condense each chapter or section to no more than six parts. Then ask yourself once again: 'Do I need to read this after all?'

If your answer is still 'Yes', start by reading the sections or chapters most relevant to your needs. Do not assume you have to begin at Chapter 1 and read through in sequence to the end. Just because that suited the writer's purpose when ordering his or her text does not mean it also suits your purpose. Where necessary, re-prioritise the material and read it in that order.

● After reading a portion of the report or chapter, stop and reflect on the material it contains.

● Relate the new ideas and information to what you already know about the subject.

● Discover which parts are likely to cause greatest difficulties and develop a strategy for dealing with such problems. If, for example, you are confused by certain unfamiliar acronyms or technical terms, look them up and create your own definitions key before reading further.

- Break long chapters or sections of a report into shorter sections. Estimate how long each will take and then make these your specific reading goals. This makes it easier to concentrate on the material than if you simply decide to read until you run out of time or get bored.

- Read flexibly, using the global approach. Skim or scan to get an overview. Then zoom in and study paragraphs demanding more critical reflection.

- Having previewed the report, remember to read actively by labelling key ideas, concepts and information in the text. If you are unable to write on the book or report itself, photocopy relevant material. Having studied complex sections, re-edit them to reduce their length and eliminate information not relevant for your purpose.

- Underline any parts which require further study.

- Highlight key words and concepts in each paragraph.

Constantly zoom in and out, from overview to close study of key details and then back to overview.

6 How to read and deal with your mail more rapidly

In the course of a lifetime, people in business can expect to receive at least 50,000 items of unsolicited direct mail, also known as 'junk mail'.

Assuming it takes you 60 seconds to open and read each of these, you will have spent around 20 working weeks, or five months of your life, doing nothing else. Whether this provides a worthwhile investment of your time depends on the extent to which reading such mailings helps you achieve goals in life.

In most cases it is unlikely that more than one in 10 of such mailings will be of any genuine interest or benefit to you. If you stop reading all but that 10 per cent, your time invested comes down to just two weeks. By using the rapid reading techniques described above you can further reduce the time taken to decide whether or not a document contains information of interest from an average of one minute down to 15 seconds, bringing down the total time required to less than a week. Deal with your letters and other mail as follows:

- Open them over a waste basket so you can drop straight into the bin anything which fails to offer you a benefit.

- Handle each item only once. Decide what action to take, even if only to put it in an action file.

Batching tasks together makes for greater productivity because it enhances focus and concentration, so by placing your correspondence in an action file, and dealing with the entire contents at one go, you will greatly reduce the time involved.

- Respond by phone, either voice, fax or E-mail, whenever possible.

- Alternatively, make a brief comment on the original letter and fax it, or use a Post-It note and mail the same letter straight back after taking a copy for your records.

How to save time when writing

For many people, writing anything more than a brief memo is a time-consuming nightmare. They procrastinate and stare at the blank paper, or equally blank VDU. They search desperately, and at considerable length, for exactly the right words to express their thoughts.

They write a few lines and delete them. They begin again and, once again, feel dissatisfied with what they have written. So it continues, with time slipping past and the deadline looming ever larger.

While nothing will ever make the task of writing a report,

presentation or any other lengthy and demanding piece of copy easy, there are practical steps you can take to improve the speed and efficiency with which text is produced.

1 Be clear what you want to say

To write clearly, you must have established in your own mind the specific reason for preparing the text. This spells out the scope of your writing and allows you to bring the topic into focus, establishing your point-of-view on the subject. On occasions it may only be implied, but the more clearly the thesis is stated, the more successful the speech will be.

Is your text intended to provide information, to persuade people to adopt a course of action, or a combination of both?

With the answer to this question in mind, write a basic structure for your presentation. Having established the direction you want to take, identify the main points which will develop your thesis. These must be organised in a logical, consistent and meaningful way. For example:

- Prevention and cure
- Problem and solution
- Cause and effect

2 Prepare an outline

Without this, the text's organisation will be haphazard. An outline compels you to think through your ideas and keeps you on track. One useful exercise is to summarise your main points in no more than 50 words. This is the number of words which can be read in 20 seconds at a reasonable and easily understood rate of delivery.

- Start with an introduction. State your aims and the areas you intend to cover.
- Next, summarise the body of your text point by point.
- Finally, draw your conclusion(s), which should be clear and convincing.

One method for doing this is to write down a series of headings, each with its set of related bullet points. This lets you see at a glance the overall structure and warns you should you begin going off at a tangent.

If, for instance, you have too many bullet points under a particular heading, it could mean you are going into unnecessary detail. Perhaps that single heading should be broken down into two – or even more.

- Keep it simple.
- Keep your points clear and well supported.
- Keep it short. (This is especially true when writing a presentation to be spoken aloud, since this always takes longer to give than you believe while writing.)

3 Getting started

Most writers – myself included – agree that the toughest part is making a start. It can be even harder to know where to begin when preparing a presentation to be spoken aloud, possibly before a critical audience. Not for the speech writer the reassuring anonymity of the relationship between book author and reader! Here are 10 ways to get yourself started:

- When preparing the first draft, do not worry too much about getting the content 100 per cent correct. It is better to allow your ideas to flow rapidly on to the page, even at the expense of some sloppy sentences or poorly constructed paragraphs.

  Never mind if your copy seems disjointed or too long in the first draft. It is easier to edit material down than it is to write it in the first place.

- Maintaining a rapid writing pace helps to keep your creative juices flowing and ensures than your words will sound natural when you speak them aloud.

- Once your ideas are flowing, never stop to re-read what you have written or you may dry up. If you have difficulty knowing where to begin, just write down any thoughts related to your presentation which come to mind. While writing, vary the sentence lengths. But avoid very long sentences. As a general rule, the shorter the sentence the better.

- Still stuck? Instead of trying to write down your ideas, just speak them out loud into a dictating machine. Expressing your ideas verbally often breaks down any blocks to creativity.

- If you are writing a spoken presentation, use 'You' and 'Yours' at the start, so each member of your audience clearly sees the relevance to their needs.

- When preparing a sales pitch or other persuasive presentation, avoid using the word 'benefit' directly – it sounds too much like hype. Instead, describe the results that purchasing your service or product will provide.

- Write a list of these benefits, using just a few key words – the fewer the better. Now create a mini-pitch/report around those key words.

- While it is important to use technical expressions, where relevant, avoid jargon whenever possible. These are words included only to demonstrate how knowledgeable you are! For the same reason, cut out any words which sound pompous, ponderous, patronising or pedantic.

- Our recollection is best for words we hear first and last. It is the parts in the middle which are hardest to recall. Psychologists call this the 'primacy' and 'recency' effects. Be sure to outline your key facts, figures, ideas and arguments at the start, then summarise them again at the end.

- Banish phrases which add nothing to your message, such as:

1 'It goes without saying . . .' Then why say it?
2 'It's hardly necessary to repeat . . .' Why repeat it?
3 'I would like to begin by saying . . .' Just say it!
4 'I feel sure you will understand . . .' Don't bet on it!

Finally, keep in mind that no matter what the topic of your text, logic and structure are of key importance. Your readers must be able to follow your explanations or arguments as rapidly and as easily as the nature of the material allows.

11 | IDENTIFYING YOUR GOALS

'Year by year we are becoming better equipped to accomplish the things we are striving for. But what are we striving for?'

Dr Lawrence Peter, author of *The Peter Principle*

IN PREVIOUS CHAPTERS, I have looked at practical ways of reducing time wasting by changing the way certain jobs are done, and examining whether certain tasks really need to be undertaken at all. By applying these procedures you will save yourself significant amounts of time.

To make every second count, however, you must have a clear sense of where you want to go in life; what you want to do, to be and to achieve.

At the heart of effective time management lie specific and well-defined life goals. Without these you will never really know how best to invest your time or whether that investment is proving worth while.

Aimless drifters

Two thousand years ago the Roman philosopher Lucius Annaeus Seneca commented that, for a ship without a harbour, 'no wind ever blows from the right quarter'.

Yet, despite the importance of setting goals, the vast majority of people spend their lives aboard Seneca's aimlessly drifting vessel. They are constantly blown to and fro by the vicissitudes of fate, without any clear course to steer and with no particular destination in mind.

Instead of being able to work consistently and efficiently towards clearly defined objectives, the individual becomes a victim of chance and circumstance.

FOUR TYPES OF PEOPLE

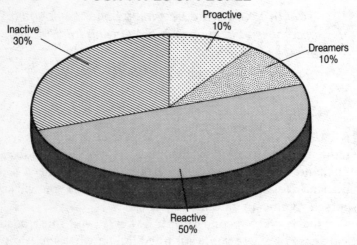

How many people fail to set goals? Research suggests it could be as high as 97 per cent of the population! One study found that some 30 per cent of the population are *inactive*: they have no goals and act only when told what, where and how to do it by another person.

Around 50 per cent are *reactive* – responding to events instead of trying to initiate change or control their destiny. They spend their lives labouring to achieve the goals of others.

A further 10 per cent are *dreamers* full of fantastic schemes to gain fame and fortune. Unfortunately, their goals are so imprecise and unrealistic they can never take the practical steps needed to make them reality.

This leaves just 10 per cent of the population who are *proactive*. Instead of waiting to be told what to do, or responding to events dictated by others, or dreaming their lives away, they go out into the world and make things happen. Instead of being content to play the hand life deals, they deal themselves a better hand. They initiate change and actively take control of their lives. They look on change not as a threat but as an opportunity.

Yet even among this select group, goal setting remains haphazard and infrequent. In a study of the Yale class of 1953, it was found that only 3 per cent had ever set themselves goals in life.

But the researchers also reported that among this tiny proportion were found the most successful men and women in every field of human endeavour. They included top business and sporting personalities, stunningly successful entrepreneurs and highly respected academics, world-class journalists, writers and artists, prize-winning scientists and top of the bill entertainers. This 3 per cent had out-performed and out-earned the rest of their class mates, often by a factor of hundreds of times.

The crucial importance of setting yourself clear goals

Most ambitious men and women acknowledge that, without goals, their life can have no direction. They agree that, despite their ambition, their failure to follow a clearly defined path through life has prevented them from fulfilling their true potential. And they admire people who set goals and work to achieve them. They also recognise that an absence of goals makes it impossible to determine how time can best be spent.

Yet, despite all this, a majority still do not set firm goals for themselves.

Why should this be? Why is goal setting neglected, even by otherwise well organised and ambitious men and women?

Below are six of the most common 'reasons' people give me for failing to set specific, written goals. If you are among those who have never bothered to give themselves goals, perhaps some of these 'reasons' account for *your* inaction.

---

1 'Who needs goals? I've not done badly in life without ever setting one.'

2 'My goals are all in my head. I've never needed to write them down.'

3 'Setting goals increases my risk of failure.'

4 'Achieving goals means others will expect too much of me.'

5 'Having clear goals robs life of spontaneity.'

6 'How can I list my goals? I want so much from life.'

So much for the excuses – for that is what they are! Now let's look at the reality:

1 'Who needs goals? I've not done so badly in life without ever setting one.'

This is the same as saying anywhere you happen to end up in life will be OK by you! It's like the airline pilot who told his passengers over the public address system that he had some bad news and some good news. 'The bad news is that all our navigational equipment has been knocked out by lightning, we are lost in a storm over the mountains and I have no idea where we are going. The good news is that we are heading there at 600 mph!'

2 'My goals are all in my head. I've never needed to write them down.'

Goals which are not written down are more accurately described as intentions. Your ambitions have to be turned into clearly defined actions before they can be realised. So long as they remain inside your mind only, you will belong to that 10 per cent of impractical dreamers mentioned above. I am reminded of the pop record producer who received a letter from a would-be composer which said: 'I have the most wonderful song which I know would be a number one hit. Unfortunately, the words and music are all locked in my head.' 'Fine,' said the producer, 'send me your head, and I'll see what can be done!'

The same applies to setting goals. So long as they remain locked away inside your skull, they are unlikely to guide your actions on a day-to-day basis. They are about as helpful in directing your path through life as a mirage would be for the traveller lost in a desert.

Most people who fail to write down their goals risk ending their days repeating the saddest phrase in any language, 'What might have been!'

3 'Setting goals increases my risk of failure.'

True enough. But will you ever achieve anything worth while either? An American publisher once asked me: 'How can I be sure that I will never publish a book that fails?' I told her the answer was simple. If she stopped publishing books at all, she would be guaranteed never to have a failure!

It is said that Thomas Edison, the great American inventor, tested 1,000 different materials for use as filaments in electric light bulbs before he finally hit on one – tungsten – which worked. Somebody remarked that this showed he had failed 1,000 times. 'On the contrary,' Edison replied. 'It means I have found 1,000 ways you *cannot* make a light bulb!'

Voicing a similar philosophy, Irish playwright George Bernard Shaw commented that as a young man he realised nine out of 10 of the things he attempted would fail. 'I therefore resolved,' he said, 'to do 10 times as many things.'

When you set yourself a complex goal – and most worthwhile life goals come into this category – the secret of success is to break it down into more manageable sub-goals which, although still demanding, you can be reasonably confident of accomplishing. By working slowly but surely towards the overall goal, you not only stand a far better chance of achieving all you set out to achieve in life, but are also far more likely to sustain self-confidence and motivation.

So be prepared to leave your comfort zone behind. Winners in life know where they are going. Losers only go where they are sent – or stay put. A rut is simply a grave with the ends kicked out!

4 'Achieving goals means others will expect too much of me.'

True. And first in line with those raised expectations will be yourself. Success, like failure, is addictive. In fact, it's the most powerful drug in the world. I remember asking the head teacher of a school in a deprived neighbourhood what was the one thing she would most like to give her children. 'A taste of success,' the head replied. And she was right. For having realised they could succeed, those children could be hungry for more. Setting and achieving specific, written goals is more than simply a way of managing time effectively. It is also essential to developing and sustaining high levels of confidence and self-esteem.

5 'Having clear goals robs life of spontaneity.'

The notion that setting yourself specific goals, or indeed carefully planning your time, somehow diminishes the quality of life is widely believed. As one disorganised US manager told me: 'I like to be open to opportunities. Setting goals limits one's options in life and removes any sense of excitement or spontaneity.'

The fact is that without goals people risk falling into the 'busyness' trap – confusing 'being busy' with 'doing business'.

As a result, by day's end they are exhausted from striving

without having much of value to show for their efforts. Setting yourself specific, written goals keeps you mentally focused and your energy levels high.

Without clear goals you will find too much time is wasted on low value, low priority tasks and not enough spent on high value, high priority ones. You will find yourself burdened down by demands which should have been delegated, or delayed, or dropped entirely (see Chapters 3 and 4).

Once your goals are established, however, it becomes possible to follow the advice which Socrates is said to have given to a traveller when asked how to reach Mount Olympus: 'Just make certain every step you take is headed in that direction,' replied the philosopher.

6 'How can I list my goals? I want so much from life.'

Of course you should be ambitious. Strive to do all you can in life, to achieve as many goals as are personally meaningful. It's good not to settle for second best. After all, second place means being the first of the last. Successful and self-fulfilled men and women constantly strive for a variety of professional and personal goals. In many ways, this is far better and healthier than being too single-minded.

The executive who sets himself, or herself, a range of career, family and social goals is approaching life in a more balanced manner than those concentrating solely on, for example, their careers.

That said, it must also be pointed out that there is simply not enough time in one lifetime to achieve every possible goal or even every desired goal. If you attempt to do so, you will achieve far less than you would have accomplished by being more single-minded, by striving for fewer and more clearly defined goals.

Some people are reluctant to make choices. Like children in a chocolate factory who find themselves surrounded by so many equally attractive options, it's impossible for them to decide what to choose and what to reject. They flit like butterflies from one interest and enthusiasm to the next, never allowing themselves enough time to accomplish very much of

TIPS FROM THE TOP

Jeffrey Archer

'The secret really is discipline. When I am writing, I write from six until eight in the morning, then from 10 until 12, two until four and six until eight. In that way, in any one year, I can do seven to eight hundred hours of writing in non-political time – basically during the holidays in August, September and in December. I have the advantage of having been an international athlete and you get used to training to be fit in body and mind. You get used to that sort of discipline.

'Even when I am not writing, for example when I was working for Margaret Thatcher, I worked in the same way – eight hours split into four intensive blocks of two. As far as writing goes, my diary is already booked for two years. I know which 16 weeks I will be writing to that programme. Whatever I'm doing, writing or making political speeches or whatever, I stick to my timetable. You have to be ruthless. For example, yesterday I was having lunch with old friends but I left them on time according to my schedule, leaving them to enjoy a thoroughly good afternoon.

'I don't waste time. A lot of people spend a lot of time doing nothing, on chit chat, making phone calls, drinking coffee, reading the paper. That's all very well but I like to be able to account for what I've done in that two hours. To feel I've achieved something.

'Of course, I also take time for leisure and exercise, and I am fortunate enough to be married to a woman who has an equally punishing schedule and is just as ruthless with time.'

anything. Far from leading to contentment, this is more likely to result in frustration, disappointment and a sense of failure. As novelist William James commented: 'There is no more miserable human being than one in whom nothing is habitual but indecision.'

I have stressed the importance of creating and working

towards clear goals in life because I regard this as absolutely fundamental to successful self and time management. Indeed, if you were to adopt no other procedure from this book except for a determination to establish life goals, you would already be halfway to becoming an excellent manager of time. Since your life span is limited, there is no option but to be selective, to focus clearly on the things which matter most to you, and to make your own choices rather than have others force their choices on you.

The importance of setting, establishing and working towards clear goals in a highly disciplined manner is illustrated by the comments on the opposite page on his approach to effective self-management by the millionaire writer Jeffrey Archer.

Setting your goals

You see a house on fire. Smoke is billowing from the windows and somebody is lying unconscious by the open front door. In such an emergency, your goals are obvious:

1 Save life by pulling the victim to safety.

2 Put out the blaze by calling the fire brigade.

Clear goals such as these mean that no time is wasted.
Unfortunately, there are few other occasions when the situation is as clear cut. Mostly, our goals seem vague, hard to define or to measure.

- 'I'd like to be happier in my work.'

- 'I really should get fitter.'

- 'I wish my relationship was working out better.'

- 'I long to make friends more easily.'

- 'I want fast promotion.'

- 'I would enjoy being able to speak another language.'

However worthy these may seem, they are not true goals – merely ill-defined ambitions.

Another difficulty may be that goals conflict with one another. For instance you want to spend more time with your family but also to carve out a successful career.

At work there may be conflicts between your goals and what your superiors will allow you to achieve!

Three types of goals

All goals come into one of three categories: 'Why', 'What' and 'How' goals.

1 'Why' goals are personal goals. They are concerned with your family, and relationships, your mental and physical health, your ethical and spiritual needs, and relationships with others.

They form the bedrock of your life, the reasons 'Why' you want to achieve all other goals in life. Unfortunately it is all too easy to become so focused on trying to accomplish 'What' and 'How' that you lose sight of the 'Why?' ones.

2 'What' goals describe your ambitions. They include career, financial and security goals. They are 'What' you want, or need, to accomplish in order to achieve your 'Why' goals.

3 'How' goals specify ways in which 'What' goals can be achieved. Let's see how these various goals operate:

- **'What' goals.** 'I want to become my company's top salesperson, to join the President's Club by outselling my quota by more than 80 per cent and earn £200,000 a year.'

- **'How' goals.** 'I shall achieve all this by finely tuning my selling skills. By expanding my network of contacts and prospects. By making more sales calls. By closing more deals.'

● **'Why' goals.** 'I want to achieve this to ensure my family's financial security. To enjoy recognition from others in the company and make my parents proud of me. To see myself as a success and feel good about achievements. To live in a nice neighbourhood, and to give my children the best possible start in life.'

As you can see, these 'Why' goals are the driving force behind all our other goals, which makes them our most personal and important goals.

People who focus too narrowly on 'What' or 'How' goals, without ever getting their 'Why' goals clear in their heads, risk ending their days disillusioned and despairing, no matter how successful the outside world considers them to be.

The man or woman who labours for years to achieve the 'What' goal of making a fortune, without ever asking, 'Why am I trying to do this?', is doomed to disillusionment even when their ambition has been achieved. Without an understanding of 'Why', all victories are hollow.

In the 1980s' movie *The Prisoner of Fifth Avenue*, Jack Lemmon played an advertising executive whose extravagant lifestyle crumbled after he was made redundant. Returning home, he discovers that thieves have ransacked and trashed his luxurious New York apartment. Sitting disconsolately amid the wreckage, he salvages a musical corkscrew and reminds himself: 'I invested two hours of my life to buy this!', realising in that instant that his life's work and achievements were a sham.

By focusing too intensely on his 'What' goals he had lost sight of his far more significant 'Why' goals.

Identifying your 'Why' goals

A good way of identifying 'Why' goals is to prepare your own obituary! While this might appear a macabre suggestion, it's a powerful way of focusing on those things which matter most to you in life. When doing this, write about yourself not as you are now, but as you ideally want to become.

- How do you want to be remembered?

- What professional and career goals would you hope to have achieved by the end of your life?

- What sort of relationships do you want to have enjoyed?

- Where would you like to be living, and under what circumstances?

- What sort of physical and mental shape do you want to be in?

- How would you like your friends to remember you?

- Would you like to have made your mark on society as a whole?

Use your imagination to create a memorial that you feel is a fitting monument to a lifetime of hard work and endeavour. The example below suggests how this might be done.

LIFESTYLE PLANNER

Prepare a fantasy obituary by completing the form below.
Include ambitions yet to be achieved.

John died last night aged _126_

in _Paris_ _(Where you would most enjoy to be living)_

John worked as a _Film producer_ _(The career you'd like to follow)_

achieving the postion of _Top Documentary Director_ _(How high you hope to rise)_

Outside work _Sailing, Painting & Travel_ _(Hobbies, leisure activities, interests)_

John's achievements included _Working to raise_
awareness of threat to rain forests

John will be best remembered for _Kindness & loving friendships_

Now prepare one for yourself, using the blank outline below.

LIFESTYLE PLANNER

Prepare a fantasy obituary by completing the form below.
Include ambitions yet to be achieved.

_____ died last night aged _____

in _____ *(Where you would most enjoy to be living)*

_____ worked as a _____ *(The career you'd like to follow)*

achieving the postion of _____ *(How high you hope to rise)*

Outside work _____ *(Hobbies, leisure activities, interests)*

_____'s achievements included _____

_____

_____ will be best remembered for _____

Ask yourself: 'What am I currently doing to achieve those goals?'

If the answer is 'Little or nothing', read the section below and then consider what changes may be needed to help accomplish them.

Identifying 'What' and 'How' goals

Some executives claim it is impractical to set specific career goals because of the importance they place on luck and chance in achieving success:

● The chance of being in the right place at the right time.

● The luck of meeting a dynamic mentor when climbing the corporate ladder.

While both *are* important to a degree, luck has accurately

been defined as 'the moment preparedness meets opportunity'. Both can be planned for:

- By specifying your goals so that you are able to distinguish genuine opportunity from time-wasting distraction.

- By giving priority to gaining, or polishing, the skills, knowledge and experience necessary to seize and exploit those genuine opportunities. Success is all a matter of luck – ask any failure!

Five rules for setting goals

MAKE ALL YOUR GOALS SMART

S – SPECIFIC

M – MEASURABLE

A – ATTAINABLE

R – REALISTIC

T – TIME LIMITED

Whatever type of goal you are considering, make certain it satisfies these five criteria. It must be:

1 Specific. Establish a mandate of how you will be spending your time. But before deciding to work towards that goal, ask yourself whether it is something you personally desire to achieve. Or are you really setting it to please or impress someone else – parents or partner for instance?

The only goals we are ever truly motivated to strive towards, and whose accomplishment brings with it a profound sense of personal fulfilment, are those of personal value, importance and significance.

Make certain, too, that your goals are balanced. Avoid

focusing too narrowly on one aspect of life, such as your career, at the expense of family or relationships. Use the fantasy obituary as a guide to those goals which are most meaningful and important in all areas of your life.

2 Measurable. There must be some way of judging progress towards your goal. The harder it is to measure, the less likely it is to be achieved. For example, the goal of 'being slim' is too vague and subjective. One person's idea of 'slim' may be another's 'plump'. However, the goal of losing 4lb in a month is not only reasonable but easily monitored.

3 Attainable. Make sure the goal is within your area of power and responsibility. Do you have all the necessary resources available? If not, make acquiring those resources a high priority goal. How dependent are you on others in the accomplishment of those goals?

Where the answer is, 'to a considerable extent', how can you be certain they are equally committed? If you are unsure about this, then make creating such a commitment another key life goal.

4 Realistic. Your goal must be something you can realistically accomplish. That is not to say that it should be undemanding. Far from it. Goals which are too easily gained offer little by way of motivation or reward. Studies show high achievers set themselves extremely demanding goals.

But whatever you attempt must be 'attainable' by *you* and within the time available.

5 Time Limited. A deadline clarifies the urgency of your goal. But make sure your deadlines are realistic and take other demands on your time into account. While it is essential to be fully committed to your goals and convinced they are important and worth while, never allow yourself to develop tunnel vision.

Because things change rapidly, goals must be equally flexible. This applies particularly to 'What' and 'How' goals, where the means by which you achieve your 'Why' goals may change considerably in just a few months. It's been estimated, for instance, that most people will have at least seven different jobs over the course of their working life. Too single-minded a pursuit of any goal can lead you to miss opportunities.

Put your goals in writing

Using your plans and ambitions, together with insights gained from the above exercises, write your goals down under three headings:

- First, those you intend to accomplish in the long term, say within five years.

- Second, medium-term goals which you realistically expect to achieve within one year.

- Third, short-term goals which you will have accomplished during the next two months.

Although there are spaces for five goals under each heading in the charts below, there is no need to complete all five. You may wish, at a later date, to go back and add further goals.

Long-term 'What' goals

By the year _____ I shall achieve the following:
(*write in date five years hence*)

1 _____

2 _____

3 _____

4 _____

5 _____

Long-term 'How' goals

To accomplish these goals within five years I shall:

1 _____

2 _____

3 _____

4 _____

5 _____

Long term 'Why' goals

I want to achieve these goals because:

1 _____

2 _____

3 _____

4 _____

5 _____

Medium-term 'What' goals

By next year I shall achieved the following:

1 _____

2 _____

3 _____

4 _____

5 _____

Medium-term 'How' goals

To accomplish these goals within the next 12 months I shall:

1 _____

2 _____

3 _____

4 _____

5 _____

Medium-term 'Why' goals

I want to achieve these goals because:

1 _____

2 _____

3 _____

4 _____

5 _____

Short-term 'What' goals

Within two months I shall have achieved the following:

1 _____

2 _____

3 _____

4 _____

5 _____

Short-term 'How' goals

To accomplish these goals within two months I shall:

1 _____

2 _____

3 _____

4 _____

5 _____

Short-term 'Why' goals

I want to achieve these goals over the next two months because:

1 _____

2 _____

3 _____

4 _____

5 _____

Writing your goals down in this way allows you to:

- Specify and clarify them. It prevents you from having vague ambitions.

- Identify all the sub-goals – stepping stones by which your main goal can be reached.

- Establish a commitment to those goals. Notice they state 'I shall achieve . . .', not 'I hope to achieve' or 'I would like to achieve.'

- Make it easier to establish priorities.

Note this important point:

- Always write goals down in the present tense, as if they had already been achieved. This programs your subconscious to achieve those goals, increases self-confidence and enhances motivation.

Consider any obstacles to accomplishment

When considering actions ('How' goals) that will have to be taken in order to achieve your 'What' goals, consider the Limiting Steps Principle (see opposite). This means any obstacles to accomplishment which have to be overcome in order to make progress. Ask yourself:

- 'What must I do/learn/know in order to accomplish this?'

- 'Whose help do I need?'

- 'Who can block my progress?'

- 'Who do I have to co-operate/collaborate/work with in order to achieve my goal(s)?'

- 'What assumptions am I making about how the goal should be accomplished? Is there a better way?'

To pinpoint any limiting steps which could prevent you achieving one or more of your major goals, complete the Goal Potentials chart opposite. If confident that you possess a particular skill, tick under the 'Sufficient' heading. When some block to progress is identified, tick under the 'Limiting Step' heading.

Now work out the steps, or sub-goals, which will have to be taken to overcome that limitation on further progress towards attaining a goal.

- Write three of your top long-, medium- and short-term 'What' goals on separate Post-It notes or index cards, and place them where they can easily be seen each and every day. Attach them to your bathroom mirror, car dashboard,

GOAL POTENTIALS CHART

	Sufficient	Limiting Step
Career planning		
Skills required		
Communications		
Teamwork		
Decision making		
Problem solving		
Coping with change		
Assertiveness		
Delegation		
Interpersonal		

telephone and computer terminal. Put the index cards in your wallet or purse. Read them regularly and imagine they have already been achieved. This will make it far easier to sustain motivation, even during periods of disappointment and set-backs.

● Take responsibility for everything that is necessary to achieve these goals. Tell yourself: 'If that is to be . . . then it's up to me.'

Some people find it difficult to list their goals in this way, especially the 'Why' ones. If you, too, find this a problem, try using Mind Mapping, a revolutionary form of creative thinking developed by British writer Tony Buzan.

How to Mind Map your life goals

For this task you will need a large sheet of plain paper (A3 or larger) and several coloured pens. There are four steps to Mind Mapping your life goals:

1 In the centre of the paper, make a little drawing or symbol to represent yourself. It can be anything you like, from a stick man to a detailed sketch. Don't worry if you lack artistic skill – this is for your eyes only.

2 From this point, radiate lines (see below) for each of the aspects of your life (family, social, finance, career, spiritual, health, neighbourhood, friendships etc.) of importance to you. Identify each line using printed letters. Make certain the words follow the line closely and do not drift away from it. Use different colours for each of the lines.

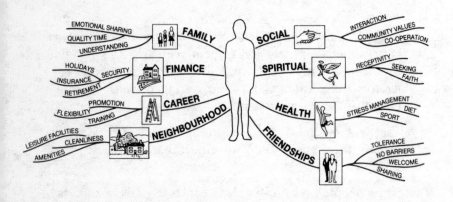

3 At the end of each line make a drawing which illustrates some aspect of that area of your life. For instance, a smiling face for friendships, an outstretched hand for social or community, a halo or shining light to represent spiritual values. It doesn't matter what you choose, so long as that sketch has personal meaning for you. Now develop each of these by extending further lines. Think about what each means to you. If your mind goes blank, free associate, writing down the first word which comes into your mind. When you think of 'finance' for example, you might bring to mind such words as 'security', 'retirement', 'holidays', 'bigger home', 'private schools', and so on.

4 Develop your Mind Map over a period of time. Keep it to hand and add further ideas, thoughts and goals as they occur to you.

This approach will make it easier to identify all three types of goals: the 'Whys', the 'Whats' and the 'Hows'. When you have done so, extract them from the Mind Map and write them down on the goal forms on page 165.

In this brief summary I have only been able to describe some basic procedures of this stimulating procedure, created some 30 years ago by Tony Buzan and widely used by individuals and major organisations around the world.

Why goals are so essential

The ability to set yourself clear goals and then plan for their accomplishment is the master skill shared by high achievers in all spheres of life. They help you to:

● Focus your efforts.
● Clarify your thoughts.
● Assist in establishing priorities.
● Improve motivation.
● Aid communication.
● Encourage achievement.

Practise setting your goals
Using the space below, write down the three goals you would most like to achieve by managing your time more effectively. These are your 'What' goals, and might include:

● Working more productively.

- Meeting deadlines more easily.
- Avoiding backlogs.

GOAL 1
_____

GOAL 2
_____

GOAL 3
_____

Next consider the main benefits from having two extra hours daily in which to 'work, rest or play!' These are your 'Why' goals and might include:

- Spending more time with my family.
- Enjoying a hobby or leisure pursuit.
- Gaining new qualifications.

GOAL 1
_____

GOAL 2
_____

GOAL 3
_____

Finally, using the knowledge gained in previous chapters, think about ways of freeing an additional 120 minutes each day. These are your 'How' goals, and could include:

- Preventing interruptions.
- Reading and writing more rapidly.
- Cutting down time wasted at meetings.

GOAL 1
_____

GOAL 2
_____

GOAL 3
_____

Setting goals is the only way to give your life a clear direction and to ensure that every second of the 168 hours available to you each week is invested wisely and well.

Setting priorities for those goals is the only way in which you can work productively and efficiently towards their attainment. In Chapter 12, I shall explain how to create a sense of order among your goals in life.

12 | IDENTIFYING YOUR PRIORITIES

'Efficiency is doing the job right. Effectiveness is doing the right job.'

Peter Drucker

HAVING CREATED a list of specific, realistic and attainable goals, your next task is to decide the order in which to work towards them. Unfortunately, getting your priorities right is not always easy. Should you, for example, place a long-term career goal above a long-term spiritual one, or rank a medium-term family goal higher than a medium-term social one?

At work it can be hard to decide which of several jobs, all demanding urgent attention, should be tackled first. As one executive told me with a note of desperation in his voice: 'Everything I do is important!'

If you are facing a similar dilemma, take some comfort from the fact that you are not alone. A survey of over 1,300 managers, including more than 500 presidents and vice-presidents, showed poor priorities setting is commonplace. Despite working long hours, less than half their day was taken up with managerial activities. The rest of the time was spent 'doing' rather than than managing.

Yet, as establishing specific goals is the only way of ensuring every second of the 168 hours available to you each week is spent wisely, so is setting priorities the only way in which you can work productively and efficiently towards attaining those goals.

TIPS FROM THE TOP

Martin Taylor, vice-chairman, the Hanson Trust

'The greatest test of time management is making your priority choices. You have to decide what you can afford to take on and what you can't. It's easy to commit yourself to something in six weeks' time simply because it seems a long way ahead. But, when you get nearer to it, you realise that other things have built up and should take priority. So you have to be disciplined about your decisions.'

How to prioritise your goals

Let's start by looking at ways to prioritise 'Why' goals, the underlying reasons for doing anything in life. They include goals concerned with:

- Self-fulfilment
- Family
- Health
- Career
- Friendships
- Spirituality

You can identify your 'Why' goal priorities from everyday actions, since those to which you have assigned a high priority are always preferred to ones with a lower priority. Here's an example of what I mean. Imagine that, after months of negotiations, you are about to close the biggest deal of your career. You are on your way to the airport to meet your customer, who has flown in just to sign that contract and has to fly out again with the hour.

Complete this deal and you will be on the fast track to top

management. You will be given a key to the executive wash-room. You will get a special award at the annual sales confer-ence. Everybody from the CEO down will praise your skills. Just as you arrive at the airport, your mobile phone rings. It's your partner calling from the hospital. Your 11-year-old child has been badly hurt in a car accident. The child is hurt, ter-rified, and crying for you. Will you:

- Immediately turn around and drive straight to the hospital, waving goodbye to the all-important contract without a second thought?

- Take the time needed to have the contract signed before going to the hospital?

Your choice when faced with such a dilemma clearly deter-mines whether family or career goals have the higher priority.

Or consider a less dramatic dilemma. This time you are an ambitious accountant who comes across irregularities in the accounts of a multi-national company where you are tipped for the top. You find large sums of money being illegally sent abroad to avoid taxes. Your department head tells you to for-get it and offers rapid promotion as a reward for your silence.

Speak out and your career prospects will be blighted. Say nothing and your conscience will never give you a moment's peace.

Will you:

- Insist on bringing the matter into the open?
- Keep quiet and enhance your prospects within the com-pany?

If you insist on speaking out, then ethical considerations clearly have a higher priority than career goals. Remain silent, and you could find your confidence and self-esteem severely undermined. Research suggests that when we make decisions which conflict with our deeply held 'Why' goals the result is emotional conflict and high levels of stress, often leading to such health problems as depression, anxiety, ulcers, high blood pressure and heart disease.

Whenever possible, therefore, it is important to ensure your 'Why' goals are in harmony with your 'What' and 'How' goals.

Creating a prioritised action list

For most people, the start of another day means facing a wide range of tasks, some trivial and easy to handle, others complex and time-consuming.

Let's suppose that a typical daily schedule involves opening and replying to letters, taking and making telephone calls, answering queries from your staff, talking to clients, preparing costings, meeting informally with colleagues, preparing a sales report, preparing for and attending formal departmental meetings and making decisions about future projects.

How would you decide which tasks will have to be tackled first and which can safely be left to later in the day?

Many priorities are decided for you. If a meeting is scheduled for 11 a.m., will last an hour and require 30 minutes' preparation, the time slot from 10.30 a.m. to 12 noon must clearly be blocked out on your schedule.

However, a sales report – which will take two hours to complete – is not needed until the following day. So you might decide to allocate a block of time between 2 p.m. and 4 p.m. to tackle that task.

But suppose an emergency arises during that period which distracts you from this task? Now you could face either working late or coming in early next day to get the report finished on time.

And what about all those other demands on your working day – the letters, visitors and telephone calls?

This is where creating a prioritised action list is helpful. It allows you to establish and monitor priorities objectively. To create this list, assign a numerical value from 1 to 3 to the two factors which determine every task's priority – its **urgency** and its **importance**.

PRIORITY = URGENCY × IMPORTANCE

- **A high priority task** is both urgent and important.

- **A medium priority task** may be either urgent or important, but never both.

- **A low priority task** is neither urgent nor important.

In the example, above, 'preparing for the meeting' probably has a high priority (the 11 a.m. deadline makes it urgent) and it is presumably important to prepare and attend.

Other activities, such as replying to letters, while important may be less urgent. It might not matter, for instance, if the letters were not posted until the following day.

Write a list of all your tasks. If you have any choice in the matter, always put each task on trial by asking yourself:

- 'Why am I doing this?'

- 'How will this help me achieve one of my goals in life?'

- 'Could I save time by doing it in a different way?'

- 'Should this be delegated?'

- 'Can it be dropped entirely?'

If the job must be done and by you, rate it on **importance** using the following scale:

1 = **Unimportant.** Would not result in major problems if not done.

2 = **Important.** Would cause serious problems if not done.

3 = **Essential.** Must be finished.

Next rate it on **urgency**, using a similar scale:

1 = **Low.** Can be done any time.

2 = **Medium.** Must be finished this week.

3 = **High.** Must be done within the next few hours.

To calculate the task's priority, multiply the two ratings. For example, a task which is both very important and urgent receives a rating of $(3 \times 3) = 9$. However, another task which, although important, was not especially urgent might be rated as $(3 \times 2) = 6$.

To get a feel for how the method works, I suggest you carry out the following exercise:

Take half a dozen of the tasks you tackled yesterday (your Time Tracker will help you to identify them) and calculate the priority of each by rating them for **urgency** and **importance**:

PRIORITY RATINGS

Task   Importance × Urgency = Priority

1 _____ _____ × _____ = ____

2 _____ _____ × _____ = ____

3 _____ _____ × _____ = ____

4 _____ _____ × _____ = ___

5 _____ _____ × _____ = ____

6 _____ _____ × _____ = ____

Tasks in order of priority

1 _____

2 _____

3 _____

4 _____

5 _____

6 _____

YOUR DAILY TIME TRACKER

TASK MANAGEMENT PRIORITIES

HIGH ▲

URGENCY ▲

LOW

A. BOTH IMPORTANT AND URGENT – **MUST DO** **HIGH PRIORITY**	**C.** URGENT BUT NOT IMPORTANT **MEDIUM PRIORITY**
1 _____ 2 _____ 3 _____ 4 _____	1 _____ 2 _____ 3 _____ 4 _____
B. IMPORTANT BUT NOT URGENT **MEDIUM PRIORITY**	**D.** NEITHER IMPORTANT NOR URGENT **NO PRIORITY**
1 _____ 2 _____ 3 _____ 4 _____	1 _____ 2 _____ 3 _____ 4 _____

HIGH ———————➤ IMPORTANCE ———————➤ LOW

PRIORITY	TIME OF DAY	TASK	TIME TAKEN	HOW TIME MIGHT BE SAVED IN FUTURE

Now complete the Task Management Matrix opposite, assigning each task to one of the four quadrants using the criteria as described above.

A. High priority: must do
Into this box go tasks rated as 3 on both **importance** and **urgency**. None of the activities listed in the other boxes should be tackled until these have been completed.

B. Medium priority: important but not urgent – can delay
In this box write tasks rated 1 or 2 on **urgency**, even if they rated 3 on **importance**. Reorganising your filing system could be a task which deserves to go here. While it is clearly important to purge redundant files, this might be postponed to a slack period. Note that **urgency** changes at short notice: for example, if a deadline is suddenly moved forward.

C. Medium priority: urgent but not important – might drop
Tasks written here will have an **urgency** rating of 3 and an **importance** rating of 1 or 2. Many of these activities, which seem so urgent at the time, are actually 'busyness' traps: demands which, while they may provide an adrenalin buzz, contribute little to overall productivity. In the next chapter I will explain how you can decide when such tasks may be safely dropped or delayed and the time put to better use.

D. No priority: neither urgent nor important – drop
Any tasks placed in this quadrant may be safely dropped, at least for the time being. You will have rated them as 1 on both **urgency** and **importance**.

The situation might change, of course, if either its importance or, less usually, urgency increases.

Photocopy this matrix, enlarging it if necessary, to provide room for all your daily tasks.

Now compare this with the information from yesterday's

Time Tracker and see whether you tackled those tasks according to their priority:

- Did you allocate sufficient time for activities which were both **urgent** and **important,** or was too much time devoted to tasks with a lower priority?

- Was the one consequence of spending too much of your time on low-priority activities not having sufficient time to deal with high-priority items?

- What time did you begin Task 1 in Box A?

- Could, or should, you have begun earlier?

- If so, how might you tackle these high-priority tasks more effectively from now on?

If you have any difficulty working out exactly how to achieve your goals, then Chapter 15 will help.

13 | STRESS AND TIME MANAGEMENT

'Death is nature's way of telling you to slow down.'
Graffiti in doctor's waiting room

THE STORY Peter told me at one of my stress and time management workshops is all too common among today's hard-pressed executives.

After recessionary cutbacks decimated the ranks of his company's managers, he found himself struggling to cope with three times his previous workload. As stress increased, Peter's mental and physical performance declined. He felt constantly tired, irritable, anxious, demoralised and depressed. He argued with his colleagues, was brutal with subordinates and fought with his family.

A victim of 'hurry sickness'

His inability to concentrate meant Peter found it difficult to make decisions, and a series of errors meant work had to be redone. This led to further increases in stress, as deadlines were missed, the backlog of uncompleted assignments grew and his position in the company became precarious. Not surprisingly, Peter's confidence and self-esteem declined sharply. At the end of a long, sleepless night he could hardly drag himself out of bed to start another dreary day. His doctor prescribed tranquillisers and anti-depressants. A psychologist advised relaxation and meditation. Peter self-prescribed several large whiskies and 60 cigarettes daily. Nothing seemed to work.

As with all victims of chronic stress, Peter had become trapped in the cycle of failure, illustrated below. Here, poor time management – caused by inadequate performance – results in increased stress, producing a further decline in performance. And so the cycle is repeated.

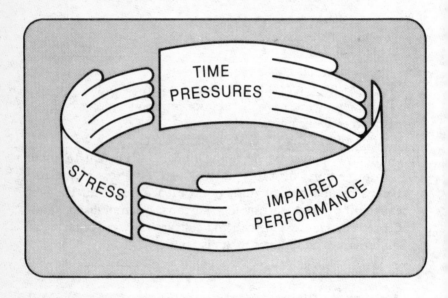

At the age of 50, when he might have expected a seat on the board, this former high flyer was forced into early retirement, one step ahead of being dismissed. Yet another victim of 'hurry sickness', the 20th-century plague whose symptoms include:

● Never having enough time in the day to meet all the demands made on you.

60-SECOND STRESS TEST

Are you a victim of hurry sickness? Take this 60-second test and find out.
Without looking at your watch, or silently counting seconds, estimate the passing of one minute. When you think time is up, check how much has actually elapsed.

What your result reveals:

● **Less than 55 seconds.** You are a victim of 'hurry sickness', and the less time which elapsed the more serious is your condition. But do not be too concerned. The practical procedures described in this book will help you to reduce that needless stress by managing your time more effectively.

● **Between 55 and 65 seconds.** Although you do not, generally, suffer from 'hurry sickness', you may still find there are too few hours in the day to accomplish all you want or need to achieve. If so, the practical procedures described in this book will allow you to gain greater control of your life.

● **More than 66 seconds.** You have a relaxed attitude to the passing of time, and dislike having to race against the clock. The greater the elapsed time, the less likely you are to suffer from the symptoms of 'hurry sickness'.

● Feeling angry and frustrated by delays, however unavoidable.

● Attempting to do everything at the double.

● Difficulty winding down once you arrive home.

● Inability to relax even on holiday.

● Lack of patience when dealing with people less fast paced than yourself.

- Leaving things to the next minute.

- Needing a 'deadline high' to motivate you.

Hurry sickness is also associated with serious health problems, including high blood pressure, ulcers, strokes and heart disease.

So what can be done to break free from this vicious and potentially fatal cycle?

Some of the remedies Peter tried, such as relaxation and meditation, can prove beneficial. But for them to reduce stress, you must also take positive steps to bring time under greater control. Only in this way can you hope to achieve that essential balance between the demands and rewards of career, family, friends, leisure pursuits and social activities.

This is not to say you should strive to create life without stress. Even were this achievable – which it is not – such an existence would be wholly undesirable. By learning to achieve the right level of mental and physical arousal, you can enhance both health and performance – for the good news is that, while excessive stress slays, the right amount merely stimulates.

Stress can be good for you!

Centuries ago the word 'stress' described the type and amount of physical torture required to extract a confession. Medieval inquisitors used thumbscrews to exert compression stress, the rack produced tensile stress while the Iron Maiden's spikes applied sheer stress!

Today most people continue to regard stress as a form of torture. The truth is that stress can be either your friend or your foe. When used correctly, stress releases hidden reserves of creative energy, enabling you to enjoy a healthier, happier and even more fulfilling life.

Peak performance stress level

Some years ago, Yuri Hanin, a Russian sports psychologist, suggested athletic success was associated with an optimal level of mental and physical alertness. Today, not only has this been widely accepted for athletes but it is recognised as holding one of the keys to achievement in all spheres of life.

We each have a level of alertness at which mind and body function best. I call this our Peak Performance Stress Level (PPSL):

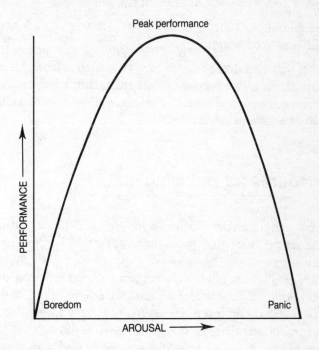

- **When there is too little stress** in our life, we feel bored, apathetic and lacking in motivation. In this state of mind, time seems to slow to a snail's pace.

- **Too much stress**, by contrast, produces anxiety, confusion and a sapping of self-confidence. In this mental state time often rushes past, making it hard to complete tasks, solve problems or make decisions.

- **At our peak of alertness** (PPSL) we feel energetic, enthusiastic, confident and, above all, in control of events.

In the future, when faced with a task which offers too little stimulating stress, consider these ways of increasing your level of alertness:

- Break a major task into smaller ones which you can complete more quickly and easily.

- Do it during your biological prime time, when you will be able to focus all your energy on the challenge.

- Delegate those aspects of the job which you consider especially unstimulating.

- See if you can do the same task to a higher level, so as to introduce a greater sense of challenge. But this should only be done when the greater demands allow you to achieve your goals more effectively.

Procedures for reducing stress

On tasks where anxiety causes a loss of confidence and poor performance, use the procedures described opposite to reduce stress.

Managing stress effectively requires an insight into those situations which prove most difficult to handle, whether these are handling confrontations, asserting yourself, negotiating, flying, public speaking or disciplining subordinates.

Sometimes the most stressful situations and activities are painfully apparent. At other times you may not be able to decide exactly what it was about a particular activity, person or circumstance that created so much stress.

One client of mine, for example, was baffled by how tense and afraid she became in the presence of her new manager. It was only after analysing her feelings carefully that she realised the woman reminded her of a particularly disagreeable teacher who had made her school life a misery.

Another middle-aged executive, by keeping the Stress Diary described below, was able to pinpoint the cause of stress in certain situations as a fear of being humiliated in front of others. This he traced back to an incident in his first job, when a sarcastic boss had regularly ridiculed him before junior staff.

Managing stress effectively requires an understanding of six key factors:

1   Awareness.   This ensures unhelpfully high levels of stress are identified at the earliest possible stage in their development. Awareness is often enhanced by keeping a written record – if you are uncertain of why a particular situation or individuals make you anxious, you can gain greater insight into your feelings by keeping a 'stress diary'. For five days record all stressful events, activities and situations which make you feel especially stressed. Details should include:

● **Date and time.**   You may discover that you are more vulnerable to stress at certain times of the day. This could coincide with a dip in your biological rhythms. if so, rescheduling the task to prime time may reduce stress.

● **Situation.**   Stress may be due to the presence of a sarcastic colleague or short-tempered boss. Certain surroundings, such as a conference room or busy office, may make you feel uneasy.

● **Feelings.**   Note down your thoughts and bodily sensations (anxiety and dry mouth or rapidly beating heart).

● **Intensity of feelings.**   Rate these on a scale of 1–5, where 1 = slight feelings of stress and 5 = highly stressed and unable to perform properly.
   For example:

Stress Diary: Alex

Date & Time: Monday 7 May – 10.25 a.m.

Situation: In the office. Wondering how to fit in all my appointments. Aware of noise of typewriters and phones.
Boss tells me to finish an urgent report by lunchtime. I try to explain this is impossible but objections brushed aside.

Feelings: Anger and resentment.

Intensity of my feelings: 4

Photocopy the sample diary page below, or copy the headings on to index cards which can be taken around with you.

Stress Diary:

Date & Time:

Situation:

Feelings:

Intensity of my feelings:

---

2 Anticipation. The diary helps you to anticipate stressful situations which can then be rehearsed in your mind's eye before the actual event. When done in a physically relaxed state, such rehearsals make it easier to deal with the event more successfully in real life. Make these rehearsals as detailed as possible. Try to hear and feel the scene being imagined, instead of merely visualising it. Picture yourself dealing with the challenge calmly and confidently.

3 Avoidance. We can liken our ability to cope with stress to having money in the bank. Each time we pay out, the funds become depleted. Being constantly in the red on our stress account is as damaging to health as being continually overdrawn at the bank would be to our financial fitness. By avoiding situations where you will become stressed to no purpose, you can conserve these limited resources.

4 Appraisal. It is not always the work you do which makes you stressed but the effort invested. We may experience great stress attempting to complete projects and meet a self-imposed deadline. At the end of the day, having raced to get things done, we go to bed worrying whether we shall get enough sleep to keep going the next day. By changing priorities and managing time more effectively, 'hurry sickness' can be more easily prevented.

5 Assertiveness. Involves protecting your own legitimate rights while respecting those of others. The secret of being assertive is confidence, self-esteem and the ability to communicate your true feelings in a relaxed and honest manner.

Unassertive people tend to impose needless stresses on themselves by taking on other people's responsibilities: always saying 'Yes' from a fear of not being liked; striving too hard to please, or attempting to live up to unrealistic expectations.

6 Action. Even when people are aware of stressful events they often do little to change the situation. A recent study found that while 72 per cent of males and 40 per cent of females admitted to being chronically stressed, few made any attempts to change their lifestyles. The most likely consequence was to ask their GP for tranquillisers or self-medicate with alcohol. Unless stress is dealt with constructively, there is a real risk that – as in the case of Peter – it can develop into a chronic condition. This has been termed burnout stress syndrome or BOSS.

Burnout is technically defined as a 'psychological withdrawal from work in response to excessive stress or dissatisfaction'. The condition leads to some or all of the following symptoms:

- Exhaustion – loss of energy, debilitation, fatigue.

- Distrust and cynicism, making it harder to maintain close personal relationships.

- Irritability, difficulty coping with minor frustrations, focusing on failure rather than successes.

- Depression, low morale and a sense of hopelessness. Loss of confidence and low self-esteem.

- Health problems, including upset digestion, aching muscles, especially in the lower back and neck; headaches, and missed menstrual periods.

- Increased consumption of cigarettes.

- Increased consumption of alcohol and drugs, both medically prescribed and otherwise.

Once established, BOSS becomes a self-reinforcing process, as the negative attitudes and actions which result lead to further discouragement and withdrawal.

Test your response to time pressures

Spend a morning or afternoon without your watch. Choose a day when you do not have any tightly scheduled meetings and are free to organise your time more or less as you wish. If your current workload makes it impossible to find any morning or afternoon which allows you freedom, find at least an hour or so when you are able to take this test. Having spent the available time without your watch, complete the assessment by ticking the appropriate statements:

1 When not wearing my watch, I felt:
(a) Much less in control of my workload.
(b) Somewhat less in control.
(c) Neither more nor less in control.
(d) Somewhat more in control.
(e) Much more in control.

2 When not wearing my watch, I felt:
(a) Much more anxious.
(b) Somewhat more anxious.
(c) Neither more nor less anxious.
(d) Somewhat less anxious.
(e) Much less anxious.

3 When not wearing my watch, I felt:
(a) Much more stressed.
(b) Somewhat more stressed.
(c) Neither more nor less stressed.
(d) Somewhat less stressed.
(e) Much less stressed.

4 When not wearing my watch, I got:
(a) Much less work done than usual.
(b) Somewhat less work done.
(c) Neither more nor less work done.
(d) Somewhat more work done.
(e) Much more work done.

Score by awarding 5 points for each **(a)** response; 4 for a **(b)**; 3 for a **(c)**; 2 for a **(d)** and 1 for an **(e)**. This gives a possible maximum score of 20 points.

What your score indicates

Score 15–20. Habit and routine play a considerable role in your management of time. Reflect on why you do certain things at certain times of the day. Is this pattern imposed from outside or one which you have freedom to change? If the latter, then consider ways in which your schedule might be adjusted or modified to improve your management of time and so reduce time related stress.

Score 9–14. Habit rather than effective time management is exerting a certain amount of influence over the way your workload is currently being organised. This could be causing you unnecessary stress. Use the information gained from your Time Tracker to identify changes that would reduce stress and improve efficiency.

Score 0–8. You do not seem to be overly pressured by the constraints of the clock. This is a good basis on which to develop more effective time and stress management procedures.

No matter what you score, this exercise helps point you towards more natural work rhythms, while increasing your awareness of the role time plays in your life.

Over the next few days try to rearrange your daily routine. Here are a few suggestions for ways this can be done. Your ability to implement them will, of course, depend on the amount of freedom and flexibility you enjoy at work:

● If possible, arrive earlier or leave later. Quiet periods before others arrive, or after they have left, can prove highly productive since interruptions are reduced or eliminated.

● Take lunch at a different time. Eating out earlier or later means a faster service and less stressful congestion. Even eating sandwiches at a different time and in a fresh venue can be relaxing.

● Using knowledge of your prime time, always try to schedule important appointments, challenging meetings, preparing or making difficult presentations and so on, for periods in the day when you are at your mental and physical peak.

Twelve ways to bring stress under control

1 Change your viewpoint

- Refuse to allow others to stress you. View rudeness or sarcasm as personality defects, which are their problem rather than a reflection on your abilities.

- Never bear grudges. As John Kennedy said: 'Forgive your enemies. Just never forget their names!'

- Say something nice to another person at least once a day. Paying compliments makes two people feel good.

- Imagine how you will feel about this situation in six months' or six years' time.

- Adopt the philosophy that 'nothing in life matters very much, and most things do not matter at all!'

2 Put your problems into perspective
Everybody has a problem, is a problem or lives with a problem! Few problems are truly catastrophic.

- Break big problems into smaller ones and solve these one at a time.

- Be optimistic. Regard mistakes and set-backs as opportunities to learn. Always try to discover something good in whatever happens to you, no matter how bad it appears at first sight.

3 Laugh at life
Studies show nursery-age children laugh an average of 450 times each day; adults only 15 times a day.

- Become childlike in your sense of fun and ability to see the ridiculous side of human experience.

4 Stop worrying – start working

'Worry' comes from an Anglo-Saxon word meaning to *strangle* or *choke*, and it prevents you from thinking or acting effectively.

One of the worst times for worrying is in the early hours of the morning, when everything seems at its bleakest and blackest. This is a time when our metabolism runs slow, body temperature is at its coolest and blood glucose level low. This physical slowing down, produced by our body clock, contributes significantly to the sense of despair and hopelessness many experience. Napoleon once remarked that he had never yet to meet a soldier with 'three o'clock in the morning courage'. So take some comfort, the next time you wake up in a pit of misery, that it is all largely biological and you will feel better and brighter when daylight arrives.

- Instead of tossing and turning, distract yourself by listening to soothing music, reading an amusing book or carrying out the relaxation exercise described in Point 7 below.

  Worry is a misuse of imagination, since studies show most of the things which worry us either never happen or are beyond our powers to control.

- So stop fretting and, where possible, start working to change the situation you find intolerable.

- As Ralph Waldo Emerson said: 'Do the thing you fear most, and the death of fear is certain.'

5 Stop talking yourself down

Be careful of what you say to yourself. Self-deprecating comments and gloomy inner dialogues undermine confidence and create needless stress.

- The next time you start telling yourself how useless you are, do a reality check. Ask whether these ideas are based on accurate facts or dubious assumptions.

- Say positive, confidence-boosting things to yourself. The idea, first popularised in the 19th century by French psychologist Emile Coué, of repeating: 'Every day, in every way, I'm getting better and better!' makes good sense.

- When you do well, congratulate yourself.

- When you blunder, look for any good points in what you did as well as the mistakes.

- Never use global terms to describe your behaviour. If you have failed to achieve a goal, tell yourself: 'I didn't succeed this time, but I know what I did wrong. Next time I'll get it right.' Instead of saying: 'This proves I will always fail.'

6 Slow your life down

Studies have shown that, as societies become more affluent and commercialised, their pace of life picks up. Everything from shopping to talking and walking is done more rapidly. The high-pressured Japanese move fastest of all, closely followed by North Americans, the English, Taiwanese and Italians. Slower movers are the Indonesians.

Even if you love life in the fast lane, your mind and body need changes in pace. In the evenings, at weekends, on short breaks or longer holidays you must learn to slow down. Here are a few suggestions for changing gear:

- Take up a hobby which cannot be rushed. Try cooking, painting, model making, gardening, pottery, juggling.

- Instead of jogging, take a stroll in the country, or your local park, deliberately pausing every so often to look at the view.

- Rather than playing a hard, competitive game of squash, golf or tennis, choose a sport which has little or no element of competition, except perhaps against nature. Go sailing or canoeing. Enjoy a leisurely swim.

- Read a non-work-related book.

- Study yoga and meditation. Increasingly, stressed executives are discovering that the powers of Eastern philosophy can offer genuine benefits in the world of business. By calming mind and body, they not only reduce stress, but make it easier to solve problems and reach decisions. One firm advocate is Ed McCracken, CEO (chief executive officer) of Silicon Graphics, a rapidly expanding computer company with annual sales of $1.5 billion. He has been meditating daily for the past 10 years. He says meditation helps by giving him greater confidence to 'let go of the feeling that I have to control everything'.

Here are some ways to centre your mind.

- Sit alone in a quiet room for five minutes and try to remain perfectly still.

- Concentrate on a single image or thought.

- When intruding ideas come into your mind simply notice them, then return to your chosen thought. You will find this a challenging exercise at first, but it will become easier with a little practice.

Slowing time down on a regular basis will make it easier for you to survive life in the fast lane.

7 Take care of your breathing and posture

One of the fist things which happen when we become stressed is that our breathing gets faster and shallower, so that only the upper portions of the lungs are used. This can produce a wide range of distressing symptoms, including: a rapidly beating heart; chest pains; dizziness, anxiety and an inability to concentrate. Deep, rhythmical, stress-reducing breathing depends on having your weight evenly distributed and taken through the spine and legs while standing and the spine and pelvis if sitting.

Disturbing this balance creates a barrier to efficient breathing.

If, for example, you have got into the habit of slouching across the steering wheel while driving or over your desk when working, most of your weight will be supported by your elbows and shoulders. This forces them to tense up and become unnecessarily involved in drawing air into your lungs.

By pushing your digestive tract upwards, such a posture also restricts the movements of diaphragm and lower ribs, making your breathing more tiring and less efficient.

Once poor posture has become a habit, lung efficiency is significantly impaired and your ability to cope with excessive stress decreases.

Emotions, especially those which you bottle up, can also have a profound effect on your breathing, especially when considerable self-control is required to keep them suppressed. This tenses chest and abdominal muscles, pulling the breastbone up and rib cage downwards. In order to breathe under these conditions, your shoulder and neck muscles have to work harder to overcome the downward force.

Because poor posture is easily overlooked, until something painful – such as a slipped disc or sore neck – reminds us, it's important to use some kind of external triggers to prompt us to consider how we are sitting or standing. This might be the ringing of your telephone or a break between finishing one task and starting another. While driving, the posture cue could be stopping at traffic lights.

Each time this happens focus attention on your posture, altering it, if necessary, to distribute your weight more evenly.

Train yourself to breathe efficiently and in a stress-reducing manner by carrying out the following exercise at odd moments during the day. It can also be used to help you relax as tension rises or to reduce fatigue at the end of a long drive, or after working at a computer:

● Sit comfortably upright and close your eyes.

● Place one hand on your chest and the other on your stomach.

- Breathe in, slowly and deeply, through your nose.

- As you exhale, consciously pull in your abdominal muscles, using your hand to push down your stomach.

- Repeat 11 more times.

Carry out this exercise for a few minutes each day until it becomes your normal pattern of breathing, whether sitting, standing or lying down.

8 Soothe away your stress

Massage is a simple, natural way of reducing stress by easing tense muscles. The following exercise will help combat mental and physical fatigue after driving, flying, or performing work which has demanded great concentration:

- Place the first fingers of each hand at either side of your nose, directly below the inner ends of each eyebrow.

- Apply a firm pressure for 10 seconds.

- Using your fingertips, very gently massage around the eyes, in a circular motion.

- Repeat three more times.

- Using your thumbs, apply a gentle pressure to the inner portion of the eyebrow arch, moving outwards from the bridge of your nose.

- Apply fingertip pressure either side of your temple. Starting at the nose make a series of circular movements across your brow, across the temple and then back around the cheekbone.

- Complete by rubbing your hands briskly together, then place them lightly over your eyes and forehead. Feel warmth from your hands flowing into your eyes and face, easing away any lingering tensions.

9 Defeat flying stress

Aircraft are dehydrating, stuffy, filled with **positive ions**. These electrically charged particles, which are also around in great numbers immediately before a thunder storm, increase the body's production of a substance called serotonin. This hormone makes us feel aggressive, irritable, moody and tired.

Negative ions, which can be found in mountains, among pine forests, beside the ocean, near waterfalls or fast flowing water, produce a sense of energy and well-being.

The recycled air inside an aircraft causes further problems. Fresh air is pumped into the cabin from the front, which means that the flight deck, first and business class areas enjoy the best of the atmosphere. The further aft one goes, the worse air quality becomes.

Here are 12 ways of defeating flying stress and reducing the effects of jet-lag, both in the air and on arrival.

In the air

- When flying on business, if possible travel business or first class. This enables you to use club lounges which are less crowded and often have fresher air. You can also save time by working more productively in tranquil surroundings.

- When travelling by coach, spend a few minutes every hour as far forward as possible.

- Take exercise by standing up, and first slowly raising and then lowering yourself on your toes. Repeat this action 10 times, placing your weight first on one leg and then the other.

- Drink plenty of water but avoid alcohol or carbonated drinks.

- If you want to sleep, eat a high carbohydrate meal such as pasta.

- If you want to stay awake eat protein, such as fish, fowl or meat, eggs, dairy products and beans. By stimulating the activity-promoting adrenalin pathway, these foodstuffs provide up to five hours of long-lasting energy.

- After a night flight, breakfast on a high protein snack such as cheese, nuts, or beans.

- For an evening meal, choose the vegetarian menu or at least avoid the meat.

- Avoid tea and coffee for a day before the flight to clear your system. Then have two cups on the morning of your flight when travelling West, or in the evening if travelling East.

On arrival

- Go to the nearest park or green space. If it has a fountain or large area of open water, even better. In the countryside, climb the nearest hill, or find running water. If you are staying by the sea, stroll along the beach. All these surroundings are rich in restful negative ions.

- In your hotel room, open the windows whenever possible. If you can neither open a window nor leave your room, have a warm – not hot – shower rather than a bath. Showers also generate negative ions.

- Many professional travellers now carry a portable ioniser with them for use in hotel rooms. These devices, smaller than a paperback book, will work in almost any country provided suitable adaptors are used. They help to reduce stress by boosting energy levels and ensuring a better night's sleep.

10 Unwinding at the day's end

This simple exercise is a great way to wind down either before starting for home, or when you've returned there at the end of a stressful day.

- Sit down, relax, half close your eyes, and focus on a spot on the ground a few feet in front of you.

- Breathe slowly and deeply while concentrating on this spot.

- Try to focus only on the spot for a full 60 seconds.

After 60 seconds, get up and return to your normal routine, carrying these feelings of deep mental relaxation with you.

11 Reduce physical stress with relaxation

When relaxing, sit or lie comfortably and loosen any tight clothing, such as a belt or tie. Some people prefer to relax in a darkened room but this is purely a matter of choice. The secret of successful relaxation is **passive concentration**. Focus on what is happening, without trying to make it happen:

- Breathe continuously, without pausing between the inhaled and exhaled breath. Each time you breathe out say the word CALM silently to yourself.

- Now clench your hands as tightly as possible. Hold this tension for a slow count to five, then uncurl your fingers and let them relax. Feel the tension flowing out of them and notice the difference between tension and relaxation in these muscles.

- Tense the muscles in your upper arms, the biceps, by trying to touch the *back* of your wrists to your shoulders. As with your hands, hold this tension for a slow count to five before allowing them to drop limply back. Let your arms flop down by your sides. Feel all the tension flowing away from your hands and arms and notice the difference between tension and relaxation.

- Shrug your shoulders as hard as you can. At the same time press your head back against some firm support. Hold for the same count to five. Allow your shoulders to drop and go limp. Feel all the tension flowing away from them, down your arms and hands, down your fingers and out into the room.

- Open your eyes wide as though enquiring. Hold for a slow count to five. Relax. Now frown hard. Hold for a count to five. Relax. Feel all the tension flowing away from the muscles in your face.

- Take – and hold – a deep breath. Flatten your abdominal muscles, as though anticipating a blow. Hold for the same slow count to five. Let those muscles go limp. Exhale with a gasp before returning to smooth, continuous breathing.

Silently repeat the word CALM with each exhaled breath. Feel more and more relaxed as your body becomes warmer and heavier.

- Stretch your legs, toes pointed, and squeeze your buttocks together. Once more hold for a slow count to five. Relax and let the muscles flop out. Now spend a few minutes enjoying the sensation of deeply relaxed muscles. As you do so, banish stress from your mind by imagining yourself lying on a sun-warmed tropical beach or in a lush green meadow beside a gently flowing stream.

If unwanted thoughts intrude, notice them in a casual way before returning to your peaceful scene.

After a relaxation session always stand up slowly and carry the feelings of relaxation through into your next activity.

12 Exercise away your stress

Moderate but regular exercise, which raises your heart rate by a modest amount, can work wonders in banishing stress and lifting depression. Walk, jog, swim, cycle . . . the choice of leisure activity is unimportant provided it continues for 20 minutes.

- **Determine your exercise heart rate** by subtracting your age from 220 to give you the maximum heart rate. Now take a proportion of this as your exercise goal. If unfit raise it by 50 per cent. If very fit, by 75 per cent.

Example: Age 20. Unfit. Maximum heart rate during exercise = 220 – 20 = 200. 50 per cent of 200 = 100 beats per minute.

Age 20. Very fit. Maximum heart rate during exercise = 220 – 20 = 200. 75 per cent of 200 = 150 beats per minute.

● **Monitor heart rate during exercise** by counting the beats in your wrist pulse for 15 seconds, then multiplying by four to get the number per minute.

Combating stress by using these 12 procedures regularly, and at the same time putting into practice the time management strategies I describe, will rapidly enhance all aspects of your performance.

14 | TIME AND CORPORATE SUCCESS

'The principle by which we live and die is that once we can do something well, we have to figure out how to do it even better.'

Donald Peterson, former chairman, Ford Motor Company

COMPANIES have long known how vital it is to manage the two key resources of **capital** and **labour** to the success of their business. Today a third no less essential resource has been added to that list – **time** itself. A 10-year study of several hundred companies has identified the management of time as the key element in corporate success:

- They found it mattered more than costs.

- More than sales levels.

- More than production or product refinements.

- It affects almost every aspect of business, from delivery to research and development, from beating the competition to addressing customer concerns.

Changing your company's time-spending ways

So far, I have concentrated on ways in which individuals can exert greater control over their own time. This chapter is specifically addressed to those of you with the authority to change the way your company or organisation spends its time. I shall explain why time management should always be one of your most pressing commitments and suggest practical ways in which this finite and fleeting resource may be exploited more effectively to give your company the winning edge.

In a single year, for example, Federal Express increased sales by more than a third, when it offered a service which guaranteed overnight delivery.

Time is also an important way of communicating corporate values to the outside world. How long does the phone ring in your office before being answered? How long to answer a letter? How long to solve a problem or make a decision?

Fifteen techniques for corporate time management

1 **Set employees clear goals.** When New York University psychologist Richard Gaits and his colleagues analysed 100 studies of worker productivity, they found setting goals improved the quantity and quality of output better than any other management techniques, including awarding pay rises and offering fleximtime arrangements.

'If you want to accomplish anything, you have to set explicit and challenging goals,' says psychologist Edwin A. Locke of the University of Maryland. 'Aiming for easy or vague goals does little for productivity. Before people can become committed to goals they have to be convinced those goals are important and worth while.'

2   Break long-term, complex tasks into short-term, well-defined weekly and daily goals.   Short-term goals make long-term goals seem more psychologically 'real'.

3   Be goal-guided rather than goal-governed.   Because the course you originally charted to take you to your goal may not always prove the most fruitful, the blind pursuit of any single goal can reduce the overall level or quality of your achievements. A goal-governed journalist, for instance, who sticks doggedly to prepared questions during an interview, may ignore a sensational revelation which is not on his or her list. A goal-guided journalist listens and thinks instead of following a question list and scribbling down the answers.

As Martin Taylor, vice-chairman of the Hanson Trust, puts it: 'I'm not a great believer in making strict rules, because your obligations are constantly changing as new issues arise. You have to be flexible.'

4   Select a project concerned with tangible, bottom-line, results rather than process goals.   It would be better, for example, to try to increase output by Y per cent or reduce turn-around time by Z hours, through more effective time management, rather than aiming for the vague and unreasonable target of 'greater productivity'.

5   Block attempts by reluctant subordinates to take refuge in doing 'busyness' instead of business by setting clearly defined targets and their accountability in attaining these goals.

6   Prepare written work plans, detailed time-tables, and explicit measurements.

7   Expand and accelerate the new time management procedures, as progress is achieved. Tackle more goals simultaneously and capture a larger share of the overall job by means of measured work plans.

8 Where appropriate, calculate a Mean Time to Response (MTTR) daily and use this as your primary measure of performance. Post the MTTR where everybody can see it.

9 Refuse to accept current levels of time performance. Think and talk about return on time as you think and talk about return on equity. Demand speed from your team. But give them the tools to achieve that increase without risking burn-out stress and the collapse of morale.

10 Eliminate non-value-added steps, that is, anything your customers would refuse to pay for if given a choice. it has been estimated that up to 90 per cent of time spent on most processes is non-value-added. Process engineers have a saying: 'Eliminate not alternate', which simply means cutting out all non-essentials. Peter Drucker says managers should ask: 'Would the roof cave in if we stopped doing this work altogether?' If the answer is 'No', eliminate that task.

When American Airlines, under Robert (My friends call me Mr) Crandall, stopped putting olives into their salads, not a single passenger appeared to notice. Certainly none complained. Yet it saved them $100,000 a year. Small changes can add up to big savings. Apply the 'Olive' philosophy to your business practices.

11 Streamline whatever is left. Look for redundancies, use technology to make information accessible after you have captured it the first time.

12 Wherever possible standardise procedures. Why waste time reinventing the wheel?

13 Eliminate backlogs, which usually make up the greatest part of turn-around time. Refuse to accept backlogs as a fact of business life. Allocate whatever time is needed to abolish them and then put processes in place to prevent their recurrence.

14 Switch to exception reporting, instead of insisting that your managers are informed about everything that happens in their particular area.

Here managers are concerned only with occasions on which performance deviates from an agreed standard by more than a predetermined amount. An exception report for a sales manager, for instance, might restrict itself to salespeople who sold less than 90 per cent or more than 110 per cent of their quota. Exception reporting enables managers to go right into the heart of problems and opportunities. They no longer have to waste time considering performances which are pretty much as expected.

The main difficulty with exception reporting lies in establishing your initial parameters. In some areas, such as production planning, sales, or budgeting, standards are always set. But they become more problematic in areas such as customer complaints, goods returned, or price variations.

Difficulties also arise when more goes wrong than goes right and exception reports, instead of being brief documents, start to run for pages.

Pareto analysis. These problems can be overcome by adopting a less widely known procedure called Pareto Analysis, named after Vilfredo Pareto whose findings I mentioned earlier (see Chapter 3).

Experience suggests that the first 20 per cent of any report accounts for more than 80 per cent of the total information it contains. So, instead of producing a bulky report, which many managers may not have time to read in detail, focus on the 20 per cent that contains most of the essential facts and figures. Such a report, which should never run to more than three pages, lists, in descending order of priority, items varying from an agreed standard by more than a previously determined amount.

A purchasing report, for instance, might include all price-variance percentages that were at least 40 per cent above or 40 per cent below standard.

Pareto analysis not only saves time in preparation and reading, but makes it far more likely that people will take in the details and clearly understand the implications.

15 Instigate the 10-Minute Time Management procedures described earlier in this book

You will find that Time Tracking alone makes a significant difference to both motivation and productivity.

Discuss the results of five days' Time Tracking, in a non-judgemental and non-threatening manner, with your staff, team, office or department. Learn from what employees tell you. Use that knowledge to initiate policies which eliminate time waste. Be as determined and methodical in exploiting time effectively as you would be in achieving the highest possible returns on the resources of capital and labour.

15 | 10-MINUTE TIME MANAGEMENT

'Listen, then be decisive.'
Sir Allen Sheppard, chairman, Grand Metropolitan

BEFORE READING this final chapter, you will need to have Time Tracking records covering five working days. This information will allow you to identify every attention shift, the time spent on every task, its priority, and delays caused by the various interruptions.

Armed with this knowledge, you can now create a blueprint for saving at least 10 hours each week (the exact amount of time which can be saved depends on how efficiently you currently use your time) for an investment of just 10 minutes a day.

Creating a time-saving blueprint

Here's what you do. Go through your Time Tracker records and rate yourself on the 10 questions below:

1 'How much of my time was devoted to low priority tasks?'
0 = Never; 1 = Rarely; 2 = Fairly frequently; 3 = Almost all the time

If your rating was 2 or 3, increase the time invested in high priority work by:

- Delegating more often and more effectively. Are you making best use of the Law of Comparative Advantage, by delegating tasks which can be done by somebody who earns less than you either do or aspire to do?

If you are a manager, avoid becoming bogged down in nitty-gritty details. Trusting your staff to handle such matters will not only save you time but make you a better manager.

Maintaining emotional distance from day-to-day tasks ensures you have more energy to deal with a genuine crisis. Your greater perspective also enables you to lead from the front instead of joining in the fray! Go through your records and tick all those tasks where time could have been saved through delegation.

- Becoming more assertive in refusing lower priority tasks. Are you saying 'No' sufficiently frequently? It is essential not to allow others to dump work on you, unless this helps you achieve a goal. Go through your tracker records and tick those tasks where time could have been saved by refusing to accede to unreasonable demands on your time.

- Dropping jobs which, while agreeable, do not help you achieve one of your goals. Put every task on trial by asking: 'Why am I doing this? How will performing this task help me achieve a goal? Which goal is it helping me to attain?' Go through your records and tick any tasks which come into this category.

- Delaying jobs which, while important, are less urgent than the task in hand. Does your Time Tracker reveal any occasions on which you mistakenly identified a task as being both **urgent** and **important**, when it was, in fact, only important? Could time have been saved by postponing this job to another time? Go through your records and tick any tasks which come into this category.

- Avoiding the mistake of tackling tasks which, although **urgent**, are not **important**. A better question to ask than:

'How can I do this job more efficiently?', is 'Why do I need to do this task at all?'

Some of the jobs which are deemed extremely urgent, and have people dropping high-priority tasks and rushing to get them done, turn out to be fairly unimportant in attaining major business or professional goals. Do not allow yourself to be led astray by the adrenalin buzz which a spurious sense of urgency often generates. Reflect, before dropping everything to deal with a supposed 'emergency', whether it is, in fact, important. Go through your records and tick any tasks which came into this category.

- Assigning priorities more carefully. Sometimes high priority jobs fail to be recognised as such and are pushed to the bottom of your 'do' list, while others, which later turn out to have a lower priority, are completed in their place. This may happen, for instance, when you make incorrect assumptions about deadlines, or the time it will take to complete a project.

For example, a low urgency task can suddenly become extremely urgent if the completion deadline is moved forward or suppliers let you down. Anticipate what can go wrong and take steps to prevent the crisis from occurring (see below).

Calculate your priorities using the Task Management Matrix. Go through your Time Tracker and tick jobs where time was wasted as a result of poorly assigned priorities. Go through your records and tick any tasks which came into this category.

Now add up the time you spent on all those items which you have ticked in response to Question One. Write this in below:

Potential time saving_____ minutes

2 'How often did I do something myself which could or should have been delegated?'

0 = Never; 1 = Rarely; 2 = Fairly frequently; 3 = Almost all the time

A rating of 2 or 3 suggests you should improve delegation skills. Even if you work on your own or in a very small office, it is often possible to delegate routine or low priority tasks by giving the work to lower cost outsiders.

Consider ways in which technology might save you time. In a small office, for example, a modern franking machine, which can be re-accredited by means of an electronic payment card or via the telephone, avoids wasting time queuing for stamps at the Post Office.

Go through your Time Tracker and tick any tasks where time might have been saved by delegation or outsourcing. Total this and write it in below:

Potential time saving_____ minutes

3 'How often was I interrupted or distracted when working on a high priority task?'

0 = Never; 1 = Rarely; 2 = Fairly frequently; 3 = Almost all the time

If your rating was 2 or 3, look for ways of reducing interruptions. Even a brief distraction from demanding tasks can cause significant delay. Avoid this time trap by:

- Arriving at work an hour earlier or working on after others have left. This also reduces wasted commuting time by enabling you to travel outside the rush hour.

- Working from home for at least part of the day. Many senior executives find this saves a great deal of time by allowing them fully to concentrate on important projects. As with flexitime, it also avoids delays when travelling through peak hour traffic.

- Suggest your department is allowed a 'call-free' period for a couple of hours each day. During this period, messages are taken but no calls are put through. The accounts departments of many major companies have implemented such a strategy and report significant gains in productivity and reductions in stress.

- If a call-free period is impossible, consider organising a rota so that each person handles incoming calls for several people for only part of the morning; this enables the others to get on with their work without constant phone interruptions.

- Discourage unscheduled 'drop in' visitors, using the methods described in Chapter 6.

- Batch tasks so as to benefit from the learning curve. As I explained in Chapter 4, you complete tasks if they require related mental skills, that is, dictating all your letters or making all your calls one after the other.

Go through your Time Tracker and tick any tasks where time would have been saved had you been interrupted less often. Add five minutes to the time spent dealing with each interruption, to take into account the additional delay in refocusing attention on your current task. Total this time and write it in below:

Potential time saving _____ minutes

4   How often did I shift priorities by jumping from one task to another?

0 = Never;   1 = Rarely;   2 = Fairly frequently;   3 = Almost all the time

If your rating is 2 or 3, consider whether the interruptions responsible for changing priorities are worse at certain times of the day or days of the week.

In some offices, for example, the phone rings constantly between 9 a.m. and noon, but there are quieter periods between noon and 2 p.m. and again in the late afternoon. If you can identify such a pattern, try to reorganise your work schedule so that lower priority items are tackled at this time.

Tick items on your Time Tracker where such reorganisation could save time, total the amount lost and write it in below:

Potential time saving _____ minutes

5 How many interruptions were of lower priority than the task on which I was engaged?

0 = Never;   1 = Rarely;   2 = Fairly frequently;   3 = Almost all the time

Unless this happens only rarely, find ways of preventing the pernicious Time Bandit stealing your day. Implement the many practical procedures described in this book. Total the time lost through interruptions and write it in below:

Potential time saving _____ minutes

6 How often did I postpone a disagreeable but high priority task in favour of something less urgent and/or important which was more interesting?

0 = Never;   1 = Rarely;   2 = Fairly frequently;   3 = Almost all the time

If you rated this 2 or 3, consider why you were tempted to procrastinate.

Was it because you felt anxious about the task or were bored to tears at the prospect of having to do it? In this case, you may have been tempted to waste time on some 'displacement' activity, in order to postpone the moment when that disagreeable chore had to be tackled.

Displacement activities are pleasant, lower priority, tasks we use to persuade ourselves, and/or others, we are being busy and productive. Human nature being what it is, we tend to be good at convincing ourselves that these tasks really have a greater urgency than the job we dislike.

Remember to put every task on trial before investing your precious time in it. Ask: 'Why am I doing this? Which goal is it helping me achieve?'

Sometimes, procrastination is caused by fatigue. You lack the mental and/or physical energy to focus on a challenging job and, as a result, find your mind wandering – not everyone can perform at maximum efficiency between traditional 9 a.m. to 5 p.m. working hours.

Some are more productive if they work from early morning to mid afternoon. Others do better by starting later and working through to late evening. Still others find they need a break in the middle of the day but can be productive during the other hours.

Having learned to read your internal clock try, in so far as this is possible, to match these natural rhythms to your working environment. If you are a 'lark', who feels at his or her brightest and best first thing in the day, tackle more demanding tasks at this time, delaying lower priority items until later in the morning.

If you are an 'owl', who comes to life several hours after the start of a normal working day, try – whenever feasible – to set aside time later in the day for your more demanding tasks. Complete the Prime Time records in Appendix Two, if you are not sure when these peaks and troughs occur.

Clearly, matching personal prime time with the demands of your job depends greatly on the degree of autonomy you enjoy.

Some people are fortunate enough to work for companies which offer considerable freedom in establishing daily schedules, while others are far more restrictive. Even so, within the limits of what is realistically possible, it is helpful to find ways of adjusting work schedules to biological needs.

Tick those occasions when procrastination led you to delay high-priority tasks needlessly. Total the time which could have been saved if you had been more focused and self-disciplined. Write this in below:

Potential time saving _____ minutes

7   How often would a task have been finished if it had been done differently?

0 = Never;   1 = Rarely;   2 = Fairly frequently;   3 = Almost all the time

Many individuals and departments get into a habit of doing things in a particular way. This routine is then followed day in and day out, unquestioned and unchallenged. A good example is the internal memo without which some managers believe their working day would be incomplete. Writing, reading and filing these messages – even when using the rapid reading techniques described in Chapter 10 – is time consuming. The question few people ever ask themselves is whether that time has been well spent. One boss who saved time and improved productivity by dumping the majority of memos is Paul Saxton, president and CEO of General Housewares Corp., based in Terre Haute, Indiana.

He actively discourages his staff from writing memos the only function of which is to justify what is going to be done and explain what has already happened. Paul Saxton prefers his executives to present their ideas, complete with financial backup, at short meetings where a decision can be taken rapidly.

If your Time Tracker indicated that significant amounts of time were taken up by a particular routine task, consider whether there are more efficient ways of achieving the same results. Total the time spent on these tasks and write this in below:

Potential time saving _____ minutes

8   How often was your time taken up by social, personal or other non-work related activities?

0 = Never;   1 = Rarely;   2 = Fairly frequently;   3 = Almost all the time

While a certain amount of socialising is, of course, essential in order to maintain friendly relationships with colleagues, customers and suppliers, beware of spending too much time on any activities not directly related to your goals:

- What proportion of your business phone calls, for instance, was taken up by chatting rather than doing business?

- How much time was spent gossiping with visitors?

- While sitting on boards and serving on trade associations may be important to achieving some of your goals, no time should be allocated to committee work or personal phone calls until late in the afternoon. This allows you to stay focused on your work and prevents other responsibilities getting in the way.

Total the time spent in this way and write this in below:
Potential time saving _____ minutes

9   How often were you obliged to drop a high-priority task in order to fire-fight on jobs which had gone badly wrong?

0 = Never;   1 = Rarely;   2 = Fairly frequently;   3 = Almost all the time

Remember that everything always takes longer than you think it will, especially if the job has never been done before.

Because it takes time to move up the learning curve, you can never be as efficient when tackling unfamiliar tasks as with more routine ones. And the same applies to every member of your team.

- One way to increase productivity on new activities is to avoid reinventing the wheel. Complete as much of the novel task as you can by using established routines, leaving as little as possible to be originated from scratch. When writing letters on a word processor, for example, set up standard paragraphs and formats which can be called on to the screen at the press of a key, so that only a minimum of new material has to be written in.

- Always allow a margin of error when estimating deadlines. Murphy's Law tells us that if something can go wrong, it will go wrong, and at the worst possible moment. Lewis' corollary is that Murphy was an optimist!

   Expect things to go wrong and work out what can be done to prevent them. The earlier problems are tackled, the simpler they are to resolve. As a Chinese sage remarked: 'Even the biggest problems were little problems once.'

- Use PERT (see Chapter 4) to plan each stage of complex projects, and make certain you are fully appraised of deadlines and any likely sources of delay.

- After a crisis, evaluate what went wrong and take steps to prevent similar problems occurring in the future.

Total the time spent on avoidable crisis management or preventable fire-fighting, and write this in below:

Potential time saving _____ minutes

10 How often did you waste 'dead time' (that is, when travelling, waiting etc.)?

0 = Never; 1 = Rarely; 2 = Fairly frequently; 3 = Almost all the time

A rating of 2 or 3 shows you are failing to make best use of those occasions when doing something which does not demand your full attention. However, this certainly does not mean you must never turn on the TV, read a bestseller, or pass the time when flying by watching the in-flight movie.

Relaxation, winding down, giving yourself time to reflect are important in achieving success. But make these goals in themselves so that you fill rather than kill precious time. Be purposeful in all you do and understand why you are doing it and how long it should continue.

Consider the amount of 'dead time' you might have put to better use and write this in below:

Potential time saving _____ minutes

TIPS FROM THE TOP

Rosemary Conley

'You have to be able to see pockets of time that you can pick up and use to full advantage. For example, if I'm being driven to London to do a TV programme, I'm often picked up at 6 a.m. As soon as it's light I start work and I'll work in the car for the full three hours until I'm dropped at the studio's door. On that journey, there and back, I can do a full day's work or more, because although I have a car phone it doesn't tend to ring as often as the one in the office.

'That potentially "dead time" time is really helpful. I can get through two days' dictation on a journey like that and if I know a journey is coming up I will plan to take my in-tray with me.'

Potential weekly time saving

Now add up the amount of time given in response to those 10 questions above. This total represents part of the potential weekly saving you could enjoy by implementing this 10-Minute Time Management programme.

Depending on how efficiently they currently manage their time, most business and professional people find this amounts to around two hours each day, sometimes more; or 10 extra hours each week. But before this programme can work for you, two steps have to be completed:

1 You must have clear goals to provide a direction in life. So set yourself a mission statement. What do you want to achieve and what are you doing to achieve it? Remember that, without goals, everything that happens to you is a matter of chance rather than deliberate intent.

2 You must know how your time is being spent from day to day. Continue using the Time Tracker to identify interruptions and delays which can be brought under control.

Three daily steps

From now on, devote just 10 minutes each day to the following three tasks.

● **Time Tracking.** This should take no more than five minutes spread over the working day. If it occupies any more of your time, then you are probably including too many details. Cut these down and use more abbreviations.

● **Time Analysing.** At the end of each working day, spend a few minutes analysing your Tracker charts and finding ways in which more time might be saved by dropping, delaying and delegating.

● **Create a Prioritised Action List** for use on the following day. Write these tasks at the top of a Time Tracker chart. Use this list to help you remain focused on priority tasks and to alert you when time is being used inefficiently.

And that is all there is to it. By spending 10 minutes at the end of each day on these tasks, you will not only make yourself a gift of at least one extra working day a week, but complete workloads more efficiently and with far less stress.

'I wasted time – now doth time waste me,' Shakespeare wrote (*Richard II*, Act V, Sc. V). 10-Minute Time and Stress Management will help ensure King Richard's sad words never become your epitaph!

APPENDIX ONE

Photocopy and use this Task Management grid and these Time Tracker forms on a daily basis.

THE TASK MANAGEMENT MATRIX

A. BOTH IMPORTANT AND URGENT – **MUST DO** **HIGH PRIORITY**	**C.** URGENT BUT NOT IMPORTANT **MEDIUM PRIORITY**
1 _____	1 _____
2 _____	2 _____
3 _____	3 _____
4 _____	4 _____
B. IMPORTANT BUT NOT URGENT **MEDIUM PRIORITY**	**D.** NEITHER IMPORTANT NOR URGENT **NO PRIORITY**
1 _____	1 _____
2 _____	2 _____
3 _____	3 _____
4 _____	4 _____

URGENCY — HIGH → LOW

HIGH ————— IMPORTANCE ————→ LOW

YOUR DAILY TIME TRACKER

PRIORITY	TIME OF DAY	TASK	TIME TAKEN	HOW TIME MIGHT BE SAVED IN FUTURE

YOUR DAILY TIME TRACKER

PRIORITY	TIME OF DAY	TASK	TIME TAKEN	HOW TIME MIGHT BE SAVED IN FUTURE

YOUR DAILY TIME TRACKER

PRIORITY	TIME OF DAY	TASK	TIME TAKEN	HOW TIME MIGHT BE SAVED IN FUTURE

APPENDIX TWO
MONITORING YOUR
PRIME TIME

For the next five days, record your levels of mental and physical energy, using the charts below – use a separate sheet for each day.

Use the negative scale (–1 to –5) to rate low levels of alertness and energy, and the positive scale (+1 to +5) for high levels of alertness and energy.

The zero line represents a mid-point where you feel neither especially energetic nor particularly lethargic.

This judgement is purely subjective and based on how you feel at each hour of the day. Complete the record by placing an 'X' in the appropriate rectangle, as shown in the example. Each square represents one hour, starting from the moment you awake and giving a maximum of 16 hours possible working time per day over a five-day period. Enough, for the needs of even an enthusiastic workaholic!

You may also find it helpful to note down any special time pressures (i.e. an urgent deadline) or other circumstances which may have increased or decreased your reserves of energy.

After a couple of days' monitoring you will probably notice your levels of physical and mental energy peak around the same time each day. These represent your natural working

WAKING HOURS – START AT WAKING, END AT BEDTIME
DAY OF WEEK: *FRIDAY*

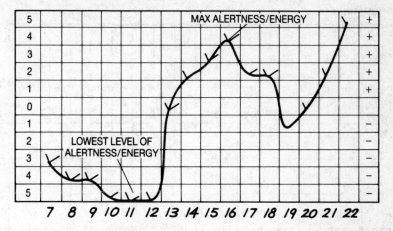

prime times. Where possible, allocate to these periods of the day your most demanding tasks, while assigning more routine chores to those times when you are mentally and physically alert.

PRIME TIME MONITORING CHART

DAY ONE:_____ (write in day of week)

Write in your starting time from the moment you get up, and then record energy levels every 60 minutes until bedtime.

Starting time =

+ 5																			+
4																			+
3																			+
2																			+
0																			
− 1																			−
2																			−
3																			−
4																			−
5																			−

PRIME TIME MONITORING CHART

DAY TWO: _____

Starting time =

+ 5																+
4																+
3																+
2																+
0																
— 1																—
2																—
3																—
4																—
5																—

PRIME TIME MONITORING CHART

DAY THREE: _____

Starting time =

+ **5**																				**+**
4																				**+**
3																				**+**
2																				**+**
0																				
− **1**																				**−**
2																				**−**
3																				**−**
4																				**−**
5																				**−**

PRIME TIME MONITORING CHART

DAY FOUR: _____

Starting time =

+ 5																		+
4																		+
3																		+
2																		+
0																		
− 1																		−
2																		−
3																		−
4																		−
5																		−

PRIME TIME MONITORING CHART

DAY FIVE: _____

Starting time =

+ 5																		+
4																		+
3																		+
2																		+
0																		
— 1																		—
2																		—
3																		—
4																		—
5																		—

BIBLIOGRAPHY

Buzan, T. and B., *The Mind Map Book: Radiant Thinking*, BBC Enterprises

Hirsch, F., *The Social Limits to Growth*, Routledge & Kegan Paul, 1977

Hodson, P. & J., *Effective Meetings*, Century Business, 1992

Levine, R.E., 'The Pace of Life', *American Scientist*, October 1990

Lewis, D., *One-Minute Stress Management*, Cedar, 1993

Linder, S., *The Harried Leisure Class*, Columbia University Press, 1970

Sherman, S., 'Leaders Learn to Heed the Voice Within', *Fortune Magazine*, pp 64–70, 22 August 1994

INDEX